P · E · R · F · E · C · T
APPETIZERS

P·E·R·F·E·C·T
APPETIZERS

DORLING KINDERSLEY
LONDON • NEW YORK • STUTTGART • MOSCOW

A DORLING KINDERSLEY BOOK

Created and Produced by
CARROLL & BROWN LIMITED
5 Lonsdale Road
London NW6 6RA

Editorial Director Jeni Wright
Editors Anna Brandenburger
Stella Vayne
Art Editor Lisa Webb
Designers Lucy De Rosa
Alan Watt
Production Editor Wendy Rogers

First published in Great Britain in 1997
by Dorling Kindersley Limited
9 Henrietta Street, London WC2E 8PS

Previously published in 1993 under the
title Look & Cook Creative Appetizers

A CIP catalogue record for this book is available
from the British Library

ISBN 0-75130-384-4

Reproduced by Colourscan, Singapore
Printed and bound in Singapore by Star Standard

CONTENTS

PERFECT APPETIZERS

Welcome to **Perfect Appetizers**. This volume is designed to be one of the simplest, most informative cookbooks you'll ever own. It is the closest I can come to sharing my personal techniques for cooking my own favourite recipes without actually being with you in the kitchen.

EQUIPMENT

Equipment and ingredients often determine whether or not you can cook a particular dish, so **Perfect Appetizers** sets out everything you need at the beginning of each recipe. You'll see at a glance how long a recipe takes to cook, how many servings it makes, what the finished dish looks like, and how much preparation can be done ahead. When you start to cook, you'll find the preparation and cooking are organized into steps that are easy to follow. Each stage has its own colour coding and everything is shown in photographs with brief text to go with each step. You will never be in doubt as to what it is you are doing, why you are doing it, and how it should look.

INGREDIENTS

❚❙❘ SERVES 4–6 🥄 WORK TIME 25–35 MINUTES 🍲 COOKING TIME 20–30 MINUTES

I've also included helpful hints and ideas under "Anne Says". These may list an alternative ingredient or piece of equipment, or explain a certain method, or add some advice on mastering a particular technique. Similarly, if there is a crucial stage in a recipe when things can go astray, I've included some warnings called "Take Care".

Many of the photographs are annotated to pinpoint why certain pieces of equipment work best, and how food should look at the various stages of cooking. Because presentation is so important, a picture of the finished dish with serving suggestions is at the end of each recipe.

Thanks to all this information, you can't go wrong. I'll be with you every step of the way. So please come with me into the kitchen to look, cook, and enjoy some delicious appetizers.

WHY APPETIZERS?

First impressions often last longest, so it is important to serve an opening dish that creates the proper mood for what is to come. An appetizer can be as simple as a salad or as special as a soufflé, depending on the occasion and your inclination. The range of recipes is wide. Some appetizers involve a minimum of ingredients and only a few minutes' work. Others may take more effort, and require some planning, but you will find that they all amply repay your attention. For light meals some appetizers can easily become simple main courses.

RECIPE CHOICE

Let the time of year help you decide what appetizer to serve your guests, with warm and hearty first courses to stave off the winter cold, or lighter ideas for a warm summer's day. Review the other dishes in your menu, and choose ingredients that will not be repeated in following courses. Take your cue, too, from cuisines such as French, Asian, Italian, and Mexican, because they will give a lively, offbeat start to any menu. Here are just a few of my own favourites.

COLD FIRST COURSES

Raw Beef Salad with Capers: the Italian classic "carpaccio" features very thinly sliced raw beef served with capers, anchovies, olive oil, and Parmesan cheese curls. *Raw Beef with Basil Sauce:* a "pesto" purée of fresh basil, garlic, pine nuts, Parmesan cheese, and olive oil is served with the very thinly sliced raw beef. *Italian Toasts with Olives, Tomatoes, and Anchovies:* crostini toasts garnished with fresh basil leaves make a quick and delicious opening to an informal, rustic meal. *Italian Toasts with Rocket and Ricotta:* peppery rocket, briefly sautéed with sweet balsamic vinegar and combined with creamy ricotta cheese, tops toasted crusty Italian peasant-style bread. *Chinese-Style Stuffed Tomatoes:* sun-ripened tomatoes of summer have an oriental filling of prawns, mangetout, and bean sprouts.

Tomatoes Stuffed with Prawns, Feta, and Black Olives: a colourful first course with a Mediterranean touch. *Stuffed Vine Leaves:* straight from the Greek Islands, vine leaves are filled with rice, pine nuts, herbs, and sultanas. *Lamb-and-Rice-Stuffed Vine Leaves:* minced lamb replaces the sultanas and pine nuts in this meaty version of "dolmades". *Chicken Liver and Apple Pâté:* this luxuriously rich pâté, complemented with apples, initiates any meal in an elegant style. *Chicken Liver Pâté with Orange:* segments of orange are a light topping for an equally rich pâté. *Greek-Style Piquant Vegetables:*

mushrooms and fennel are simmered separately with baby onions, coriander seeds, tomatoes, herbs, and white wine. *Golden Greek-Style Vegetables:* saffron gives an amber hue to courgettes, cauliflower, and onions. *Smoked Trout Mousse with Horseradish and Dill:* flakes of smoked trout are the basis for this light mousse, perfect for a buffet luncheon. *Smoked Trout Mousse with Green Peppercorns:* green peppercorns add a spicier flavour and a touch of colour to smoked trout mousse. *Blini with Smoked Salmon:* traditional Russian treat of small buckwheat pancakes served with a choice of condiments – radishes, capers, onions, and soured cream. *Blini with Red and Black Caviar:* dazzling tiny beads of caviar in contrasting colours crown more buckwheat pancakes.

WARM FIRST COURSES

Marinated Goat Cheese Salad: a French-style first course of crisp lettuces with rounds of toasted French bread topped with slices of marinated goat cheese. *Breaded Marinated Goat Cheese Salad:* marinated goat cheese is coated with breadcrumbs, and briefly pan-fried to be served with a salad of watercress and lollo rosso. *Spring Rolls with Lettuce and Mint Leaves:* crisp packages filled with minced pork, mushrooms, and cellophane noodles are wrapped in lettuce and fresh mint leaves and served with a chilli dipping sauce – an oriental favourite. *Spring Rolls Filled with Prawns:* pink prawns replace the pork in these spring rolls served on a bed of grated carrot salad. *Stuffed Mushrooms with Herbs:* large mushrooms are filled with wild mushrooms, walnuts, garlic, and herbs, then baked until hot and fragrant – a sure winner. *Mushrooms Stuffed with Sun-Dried Tomatoes and Cheese:* a souvenir of sunny Italy, these mushrooms are filled with two cheeses and sun-dried tomatoes and topped with a third cheese. *Cheese Puffs with Spinach and Smoked Salmon:* cheese choux pastry puffs make delicious containers for a spinach and cream cheese filling, which is then covered with a lattice of smoked salmon. *Cheese Rings Filled with Spinach and Mushrooms:* rings of choux pastry encase spinach filling accented with sliced mushrooms. *Poached Scallops in Cider Sauce:* scallops are poached in cider and served in their own shells with a garlic-herb potato border. *Sautéed Scallops with Lemon-Herb Potatoes:* crisply sautéed scallops partner mashed potatoes with an unusual flavouring of lemon zest. *Herbed Salmon Cakes with Sweetcorn Relish:* flakes of cooked salmon are formed into cakes, then pan-fried to be served with tangy sweetcorn relish. *Maryland Crab Cakes:* take a quick trip to the North American seashore with this Chesapeake Bay speciality. *Steamed Mussels with Saffron-Cream Sauce:* cream sauce flavoured with saffron threads coats these salty mussels – crusty bread is a must for soaking up the sauce! *Moules Marinière:* here, the mussels are simply steamed so the cooking liquid makes a delicious broth. *Clams Steamed in White Wine:* as an alternative to mussels, clams are steamed to create a great meal for friends. *Sautéed Onion and Roquefort Quiche:* piquant Roquefort cheese and caramelized onions encased in a buttery crust will sharpen your appetite. *Cabbage and Goat Cheese Quiche:* fresh goat cheese and shredded white cabbage combine in a tasty quiche. *Oysters in Champagne Sauce:* a frothy Champagne sauce covers oysters in this elegant presentation. *Oysters Rockefeller:* spinach stuffing is the hallmark of these baked oysters, claimed to be as rich as the man himself. *Red Cabbage and Bacon Salad with Blue Cheese:* a bistro-style salad of substance with a slight smoky flavour. *White Cabbage, Walnut, and Bacon Salad:* chopped walnuts add crunch to finely shredded white cabbage. *Szechuan Sweet and Sour Spareribs:* pork ribs fried in oil spiced with hot chilli are slowly simmered with oriental flavourings until glazed and tender. *Indonesian Spicy Spareribs:* ginger and other spices give fragrant flavour to the ribs during the same slow cooking. *Mexican Turnovers with Chicken and Cheese:* tortillas form a handy wrapping for a chicken and cheese filling; fried like quesadillas, they are served with spicy guacamole and tomato-onion garnish. *Mexican Turnovers with Pork:* pork joins with Cheddar cheese in the filling for these turnovers. *Parma Ham Pizzas with Mozzarella and Basil:* a classic Italian combination of tomato sauce, strips of Parma ham, basil leaves, and mozzarella cheese tops these individual pizzas. *Tropical Prawn Kebabs:* grilled prawns on skewers are transformed by a marinade of fresh root ginger, lime juice, and fresh coriander leaves, and served with a spicy peanut sauce. *Vietnamese Prawn Kebabs:* balls of puréed prawns are coated in desiccated coconut before being baked in the oven and served with peanut sauce. *Cheddar Cheese and Courgette Soufflé:* courgettes add colour and Cheddar cheese adds flavour in this special first course. *Onion and Sage Soufflé:* onions cooked to a purée and flavoured with fresh sage are the base for this heartier soufflé.

EQUIPMENT

Appetizer recipes vary widely, and so does the equipment necessary to make them. First priority is a good, sharp chef's knife for chopping. A thin-bladed, flexible slicing knife cuts paper-thin slices of meat and fish, but a long serrated knife or even an electric carving knife can also do the job. In some recipes a food processor will save a considerable amount of time when chopping and puréeing. A blender can usually be used in its place, but the ingredients may need to be worked in batches. Heavy-based saucepans, frying pans, and sauté pans are important. In some oriental recipes a wok will be the cooking utensil of choice. Individual soufflé dishes or ramekins are used as moulds or baking dishes in some recipes, other specialized equipment needed for specific recipes includes a terrine mould, a flan tin with removable base, wooden or metal skewers for grilling, and an oyster knife. A few of the recipes call for a piping bag fitted with a piping nozzle for shaping mixtures neatly, but instead you can use two spoons or a palette knife to achieve the same effect.

INGREDIENTS

Vegetables and fruits, meat and seafood, cheese, and nuts, there is no end to the amount of ingredients that contribute to creative appetizers. All sorts of vegetables appear, from garden greens, onions, and peppers to cabbage and aubergines. Some play a dominant role in recipes such as Stuffed Mushrooms with Herbs. Others form a partnership with other ingredients in dishes like Sautéed Onion and Roquefort Quiche, and Red Cabbage and Bacon Salad with Blue Cheese. Delicate shellfish – prawns, clams, scallops, mussels, and oysters – are luxury favourites, not to mention the smoked salmon and caviar served with blini. Smoked trout is used to flavour a rich mousse, while fresh salmon is formed into tasty cakes to serve with a tangy sweetcorn relish. Recipes featuring poultry and meat in this book include Raw Beef Salad with Capers, Szechuan Sweet and Sour Spareribs, Chicken Liver and Apple Pâté, and Mexican Turnovers with Chicken and Cheese. Lively, salty, and tart seasonings are often key ingredients in appetizers. Cheeses such as Roquefort, goat, Parmesan, and Cheddar give a rich flavour to several dishes, including Marinated Goat Cheese Salad. A piquant accent is added to many recipes with capers, garlic, fresh chillies, and even horseradish. Vinegar and fresh lemon juice enliven other recipes, such as Greek-Style Piquant Vegetables and Stuffed Vine Leaves. The more prized ingredients are caviar, Champagne, and saffron; they are used in small quantities to add an opening touch of elegance for a grand occasion.

TECHNIQUES

The techniques used in this book are as varied as the recipes. You will be doing a good deal of chopping, slicing, and shaping ingredients for attractive presentations. Some dishes only require little cooking, relying simply on blanching, toasting, or quick sautéing. Shellfish are rapidly cooked by poaching, grilling, and steaming. Marinating in wine or lemon juice, oil, and a variety of seasonings is a practical technique that adds flavour and tenderness before cooking. Just occasionally, as in Raw Beef Salad with Capers, ingredients may be served without any cooking at all. Stove-top preparations include the blanching and simmering of vegetables, and pan-frying of food such as salmon cakes and Mexican Turnovers with Chicken and Cheese. The oven comes into play for cooking soufflés and when baking pastry tarts, choux puffs, and toasts for crostini. You will also learn how to make an assortment of sauces and accompaniments, including guacamole, Indonesian peanut sauce, vinaigrette dressing, sweetcorn relish, and flavoured mashed potatoes. As with other volumes in the *Look & Cook* series, we describe in detail the basic techniques that are commonly used in these recipes. You will see how to chop herbs; how to peel, seed, and chop tomatoes; how to chop onions and shallots; how to core, seed, and dice peppers and fresh hot chillies; how to chop root ginger and garlic; and how to core, peel, and dice apples. Decorative ideas include how to make a spring onion brush.

RAW BEEF SALAD WITH CAPERS

Carpaccio Piccante

🍽 SERVES 4 🥄 WORK TIME 20–25 MINUTES*

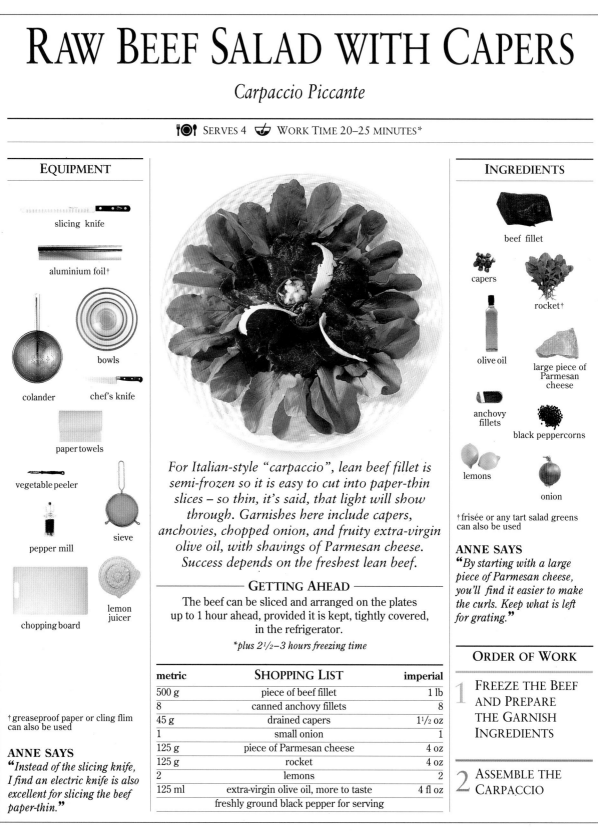

EQUIPMENT

slicing knife

aluminium foil†

bowls

colander

chef's knife

paper towels

vegetable peeler

pepper mill

sieve

lemon juicer

chopping board

† greaseproof paper or cling film can also be used

ANNE SAYS
"Instead of the slicing knife, I find an electric knife is also excellent for slicing the beef paper-thin."

For Italian-style "carpaccio", lean beef fillet is semi-frozen so it is easy to cut into paper-thin slices – so thin, it's said, that light will show through. Garnishes here include capers, anchovies, chopped onion, and fruity extra-virgin olive oil, with shavings of Parmesan cheese. Success depends on the freshest lean beef.

GETTING AHEAD

The beef can be sliced and arranged on the plates up to 1 hour ahead, provided it is kept, tightly covered, in the refrigerator.

*plus 2½–3 hours freezing time

metric	SHOPPING LIST	imperial
500 g	piece of beef fillet	1 lb
8	canned anchovy fillets	8
45 g	drained capers	1½ oz
1	small onion	1
125 g	piece of Parmesan cheese	4 oz
125 g	rocket	4 oz
2	lemons	2
125 ml	extra-virgin olive oil, more to taste	4 fl oz
	freshly ground black pepper for serving	

INGREDIENTS

beef fillet

capers

rocket†

olive oil

large piece of Parmesan cheese

anchovy fillets

black peppercorns

lemons

onion

† frisée or any tart salad greens can also be used

ANNE SAYS
"By starting with a large piece of Parmesan cheese, you'll find it easier to make the curls. Keep what is left for grating."

ORDER OF WORK

1. **FREEZE THE BEEF AND PREPARE THE GARNISH INGREDIENTS**

2. **ASSEMBLE THE CARPACCIO**

1 FREEZE THE BEEF AND PREPARE THE GARNISH INGREDIENTS

Use flat of hand to smooth foil

Pull foil tightly around beef so it will compress and be easy to slice

1 Wrap the beef fillet tightly in aluminium foil.

2 Twist the ends of the foil to seal well, then freeze until firm but not frozen solid, 2½–3 hours.

3 Meanwhile, drain the anchovies and spread out on paper towels. If the capers are large, coarsely chop them. Peel the onion, and cut it in half with the chef's knife. Slice each half horizontally, then vertically; cut across the onion to make dice. Continue chopping until very fine.

4 Using the vegetable peeler, shave 12 large strips from the piece of Parmesan cheese.

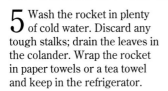

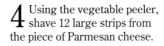

5 Wash the rocket in plenty of cold water. Discard any tough stalks; drain the leaves in the colander. Wrap the rocket in paper towels or a tea towel and keep in the refrigerator.

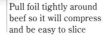

Rocket leaves will not wilt if wrapped loosely in paper towel and kept in refrigerator

2 ASSEMBLE THE CARPACCIO

1 Arrange the rocket in a single layer around the edge of 4 individual plates, leaving the centre of each plate open.

Rocket leaves make pretty display

2 Take the beef from the freezer and unwrap it. If the meat is too hard to cut, let it thaw slightly at room temperature.

3 Using the slicing knife, cut paper-thin slices from the fillet. Slice as much of the meat as you can; there will be a little left at the end.

ANNE SAYS
"Use the remaining meat for another recipe, or chop it finely to make steak tartare to serve with the carpaccio."

Paper-thin fillet slices allow light to shine through

4 As you slice the beef, arrange it, slightly overlapping, in the centre of the plates. Curl the anchovy fillets into rings and put 2 in the centre of each plate.

! TAKE CARE !
The beef is very delicate when sliced; it should be transferred to the plates directly after slicing.

5 On each serving, fill 1 anchovy ring with chopped onion and the other with capers.

Mound capers carefully so anchovy rings keep their shape

6 Squeeze the juice from the lemons; there should be 90 ml (6 tbsp) juice. Spoon the lemon juice over the beef.

7 Sprinkle the olive oil over the beef. Arrange the Parmesan cheese curls on top.

Raw beef glistens with olive oil

🍴 TO SERVE

Serve at room temperature. Pass the pepper mill separately.

Capers and onion, enclosed in rings of anchovy, add piquancy to salad

Crisp green rocket makes perfect background for beef

RAW BEEF WITH BASIL SAUCE

Pesto is a treasured sauce, concentrated in flavour and useful in a wide variety of dishes.

1 Wrap and freeze the beef as directed in the main recipe.

2 Meanwhile, make the pesto sauce: strip the leaves from 1 large bunch of fresh basil (about 90 g/3 oz), reserving 4 sprigs for garnish. Put the basil in a food processor with 4 peeled garlic cloves, 45 g (1½ oz) grated Parmesan cheese, 45 g(1½ oz) pine nuts, 5 ml (1 tsp) salt, and pepper. Purée until smooth. With the blades turning, gradually add 175 ml (6 fl oz) olive oil. Taste for seasoning.

3 Make the Parmesan cheese shavings as directed.

4 Thinly slice the beef and arrange it, overlapping, on each plate, omitting the rocket.

5 Squeeze the juice of 1 lemon over the beef and spoon a little pesto in the centre of each plate.

6 Arrange the Parmesan shavings on top and decorate with the reserved basil sprigs. Serve the remaining pesto separately.

ITALIAN TOASTS WITH OLIVES, TOMATOES, AND ANCHOVIES

Crostini alla Siciliana

🍽 SERVES 8 🥣 WORK TIME 15–20 MINUTES* ☕ BAKING TIME 5–10 MINUTES

EQUIPMENT

olive stoner

bread knife

slotted spoon

large metal spoon

chef's knife

saucepan

small knife

bowls

baking sheet

chopping board

cling film

Crostini are an Italian inspiration with an unlimited variety of toppings. Here chopped tomatoes are marinated with olive oil, basil, and garlic, then mixed with olives and anchovies. Authentic crostini call for Italian peasant-style bread, but you can substitute any crusty loaf that has a chewy centre.

*plus 30–60 minutes standing time

INGREDIENTS

peasant-style bread

black olives

tomatoes

fresh basil

olive oil

anchovy fillets

garlic cloves

ANNE SAYS
"*The choice of olive oil depends on the style of cooking. The more assertive fragrance of the better quality unrefined oils is best in these crostini.*"

metric	SHOPPING LIST	imperial
750 g	ripe tomatoes	1½ lb
1	small bunch of fresh basil	1
4	garlic cloves	4
	salt and pepper	
60 ml	extra-virgin olive oil	4 tbsp
4	canned anchovy fillets	4
150 g	Italian or Greek black olives	5 oz
1	small loaf of Italian peasant-style bread	1

ORDER OF WORK

1 PREPARE THE TOPPING

2 MAKE THE CROSTINI

1 PREPARE THE TOPPING

1 Cut the cores from the tomatoes and score an "x" on the base of each with the tip of the small knife. Immerse in a pan of boiling water until the skin starts to split, 8–15 seconds, depending on their ripeness. Using the slotted spoon, transfer them at once to a bowl of cold water. When cold, peel off the skin. Cut the tomatoes crosswise in half, squeeze out the seeds, then coarsely chop.

2 Strip the basil leaves from the stalks, reserving 8 sprigs for garnish, and pile them on the chopping board. Coarsely chop the leaves. Peel and finely chop the garlic (see box, below).

Be careful not to bruise tender basil leaves

HOW TO PEEL AND CHOP GARLIC

The strength of garlic varies with its age and dryness; use more when it is very fresh.

1 Separate the cloves from the bulb by pulling with your fingers. Alternatively, separate the cloves by crushing the bulb with the heel of your hand.

Garlic cloves are easily separated

2 Lightly crush the clove with a chef's knife to loosen the skin.

3 Carefully peel the loosened skin from the clove with your fingers, and discard. Set the flat side of the knife on top of the clove and strike firmly with your fist.

4 Finely chop the garlic with the chef's knife, moving the knife blade back and forth.

3 Combine the chopped tomatoes, garlic, and basil in a bowl. Add a little salt and pepper with the olive oil.

For best flavour use extra-virgin olive oil

Chopped tomatoes, garlic, and basil are coated with golden olive oil

Special tool makes olive stoning easy

4 Stir to mix the ingredients together, then cover and let stand at room temperature, 30–60 minutes.

5 Meanwhile, gather the anchovy fillets together with your fingers and chop them crosswise.

ANNE SAYS
"If you like, you can chop the anchovies in a food processor, and the olives too, but be careful not to overwork them or they will become a purée."

6 Stone the olives and chop them coarsely with the chef's knife.

7 Stir the olives and anchovies into the tomatoes. Taste for seasoning and adjust if necessary.

MAKE THE CROSTINI

1 Heat the oven to 200°C (400°F, Gas 6). Cut the bread into eight 1.25 cm (1/2 inch) thick slices. Spread out the slices on the baking sheet and toast until lightly browned, turning once, 5–10 minutes.

Cut generous slices so bread does not dry out too much in oven

2 Spoon the tomato, olive, and anchovy topping on the toasted bread, spreading it roughly. Garnish each crostini with a basil sprig.

🍴 TO SERVE

Arrange the crostini on a platter and serve warm or at room temperature.

Basil leaves add fresh green garnish

ITALIAN TOASTS WITH ROCKET AND RICOTTA

1 Omit the tomatoes, basil, olives, and anchovies.
2 Wash 375 g (12 oz) rocket in cold water and discard any tough stems. Tear the leaves into large pieces. Peel and chop 3 garlic cloves.
3 Heat 30 ml (2 tbsp) olive oil in a frying pan, add the rocket, garlic, salt, and pepper, and cook, stirring until rocket has wilted, 2–3 minutes. Add 45–60 ml (3–4 tbsp) balsamic vinegar and simmer 1 minute.
4 Drain the rocket in a colander and coarsely chop the leaves. Transfer them to a bowl and stir in 175 g (6 oz) ricotta cheese. Season to taste.
5 Slice and toast the bread as directed. Spread the rocket mixture on top, cut each slice in half, and serve warm, decorated with tomato wedges and black olives, if you like.

Warm toasted bread is crunchy base for crostini topping

GETTING AHEAD

The topping can be prepared up to 3–4 hours ahead and kept, covered, at room temperature. Assemble the crostini just before serving so the toasted bread does not get soggy.

CHINESE-STYLE STUFFED TOMATOES

¶❍¶ SERVES 6 ⌣ WORK TIME 30–35 MINUTES*

EQUIPMENT

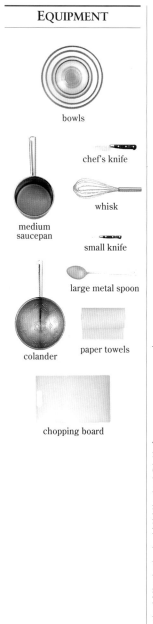

bowls

chef's knife

whisk

medium saucepan

small knife

large metal spoon

colander

paper towels

chopping board

An ideal first course for the sun-ripened tomatoes of summer. The tomatoes are filled with prawns and bean sprouts tossed in a soy and ginger vinaigrette, then arranged with a "fan" of mangetout for a brilliant, colourful effect.

GETTING AHEAD
The vinaigrette can be made up to 1 week ahead. The remaining ingredients can be prepared 1 day ahead and refrigerated. Assemble the salads not more than 1 hour before serving.

*plus 30 minutes standing time

metric	SHOPPING LIST	imperial
6	medium tomatoes, total weight about 1 kg (2¼ lb)	6
175 g	mangetout	6 oz
125 g	bean sprouts	4 oz
3	spring onions	3
250 g	peeled cooked prawns	8 oz
	salt and pepper	
	For the vinaigrette	
1.25 cm	piece of fresh root ginger	½ inch
1	garlic clove	1
30 ml	white wine vinegar	2 tbsp
10 ml	soy sauce	2 tsp
5 ml	sesame oil	1 tsp
75 ml	vegetable oil	2½ fl oz

INGREDIENTS

peeled cooked prawns

tomatoes   fresh root ginger

sesame oil

vegetable oil

bean sprouts

white wine vinegar†

mangetout   garlic

soy sauce

spring onions

†cider vinegar can also be used

ORDER OF WORK

1 PREPARE THE TOMATOES AND VINAIGRETTE

2 PREPARE THE STUFFING AND STUFF THE TOMATOES

1 PREPARE THE TOMATOES AND VINAIGRETTE

Small knife cuts neatly around core

Ripe but firm tomatoes make good cups for stuffing

1 With the small knife, core the tomatoes. If necessary, cut a thin slice from the base of each tomato so it will sit flat. Cut a slice from the top of each tomato and discard it.

2 Scrape out and discard the tomato seeds and flesh with a tablespoon, leaving a 5 mm (¹/₄ inch) shell. Sprinkle the inside of the tomatoes with salt. Set the tomatoes upside down on paper towels. Let stand 30 minutes. Meanwhile, make the vinaigrette and prepare the stuffing.

3 Make the vinaigrette: peel the ginger. With the chef's knife, slice the ginger, cutting across the fibrous grain. Crush each slice with the flat of the knife and finely chop.

4 Lightly crush the garlic clove to loosen the skin. Peel off the skin with your fingertips and discard. Finely chop the garlic using the chef's knife.

5 In a small bowl, whisk together the ginger, garlic, vinegar, soy sauce, and sesame oil. Gradually whisk in the vegetable oil so the vinaigrette emulsifies and thickens slightly. Season the dressing with salt and pepper, and set aside.

2 PREPARE THE STUFFING AND STUFF THE TOMATOES

1 With your fingers, trim the stalk end from each of the mangetout and pull the string down the pod. Trim the other end. Discard the trimmings.

2 Half fill the saucepan with cold salted water and bring to a boil. Add the mangetout and simmer until just tender, 3–4 minutes. Drain, rinse with cold water, and drain again.

3 Reserve about two-thirds of the mangetout in a bowl. Stack the remaining mangetout and cut across into 5 mm (¼ inch) slices with the chef's knife.

5 Trim the roots and coarse green tops from the spring onions. Remove any outer skin and discard, then coarsely chop them.

4 Pick over the bean sprouts and put them in a bowl. Pour boiling water over the sprouts and let stand 2 minutes. Drain, rinse with cold water, and drain again thoroughly. Coarsely chop the bean sprouts.

6 Coarsely chop the prawns, reserving 3 large whole prawns for garnish. Cut the reserved whole prawns lengthwise in half.

Whole prawns make sumptuous garnish

Chop prawns coarsely so stuffing has texture

7 Combine the chopped mangetout, bean sprouts, spring onions, prawns, and vinaigrette and toss to mix. Taste for seasoning. Lightly season the inside of the tomatoes, then fill with stuffing.

Divide stuffing equally among tomatoes

🍴 TO SERVE

Arrange the reserved mangetout in a fan on each of 6 individual plates. Put a filled tomato on each plate, and garnish with a halved prawn. If you like, decorate each serving with a spring onion brush (see box, page 99).

Fan of lush green **mangetout** forms base for stuffed tomato

TOMATOES STUFFED WITH PRAWNS, FETA, AND BLACK OLIVES

1 Prepare the tomatoes as directed in the main recipe.
2 Make the vinaigrette: whisk together 30 ml (2 tbsp) red wine vinegar, 5–10 ml (1–2 tsp) Dijon mustard, salt, and pepper. Gradually whisk in 75 ml (2½ fl oz) olive oil so the dressing emulsifies and thickens slightly.
3 Omit the mangetout and bean sprouts. Bring a pan of cold salted water to a boil, add 100 g (3½ oz) rice, and bring back to a boil. Simmer the rice until just tender, stirring occasionally, 10–12 minutes. Drain the rice, rinse with cold water, and drain again thoroughly. Let cool 8–10 minutes, then fluff with a fork; let chill in the refrigerator.
4 Coarsely chop 5–6 stoned black olives. Strip the leaves from 10–12 stalks of fresh coriander and pile them on a chopping board. With a chef's knife, coarsely chop the leaves. Crumble 45 g (1½ oz) feta cheese into a bowl. Chop the spring onions and coarsely chop all of the prawns.
5 Add the chopped black olives and coriander to the feta, with the spring onions, prawns, rice, and vinaigrette; toss to mix. Add 5–10 ml (1–2 tsp) anise-flavoured liqueur, if you like, and season to taste with salt and pepper.
6 Fill the prepared tomatoes with the stuffing, using a spoon.
7 Serve each tomato on a curly salad leaf. Decorate the plate with tender chicory leaves and fresh herbs, if you like.

21

STUFFED VINE LEAVES

Dolmades

🍽️ SERVES 8 🥣 WORK TIME 40–45 MINUTES* ♨️ COOKING TIME 45–60 MINUTES

EQUIPMENT

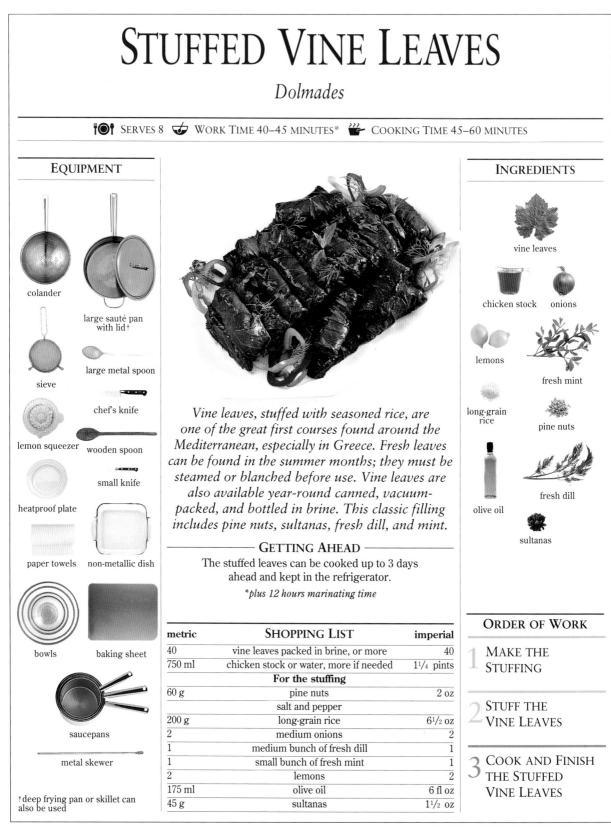

colander

large sauté pan with lid †

large metal spoon

sieve

chef's knife

lemon squeezer

wooden spoon

small knife

heatproof plate

paper towels

non-metallic dish

bowls

baking sheet

saucepans

metal skewer

†deep frying pan or skillet can also be used

INGREDIENTS

vine leaves

chicken stock   onions

lemons

fresh mint

long-grain rice

pine nuts

olive oil

fresh dill

sultanas

Vine leaves, stuffed with seasoned rice, are one of the great first courses found around the Mediterranean, especially in Greece. Fresh leaves can be found in the summer months; they must be steamed or blanched before use. Vine leaves are also available year-round canned, vacuum-packed, and bottled in brine. This classic filling includes pine nuts, sultanas, fresh dill, and mint.

— GETTING AHEAD —
The stuffed leaves can be cooked up to 3 days ahead and kept in the refrigerator.

*plus 12 hours marinating time

metric	SHOPPING LIST	imperial
40	vine leaves packed in brine, or more	40
750 ml	chicken stock or water, more if needed	1¼ pints
	For the stuffing	
60 g	pine nuts	2 oz
	salt and pepper	
200 g	long-grain rice	6½ oz
2	medium onions	2
1	medium bunch of fresh dill	1
1	small bunch of fresh mint	1
2	lemons	2
175 ml	olive oil	6 fl oz
45 g	sultanas	1½ oz

ORDER OF WORK

1 MAKE THE STUFFING

2 STUFF THE VINE LEAVES

3 COOK AND FINISH THE STUFFED VINE LEAVES

1 MAKE THE STUFFING

Toasting pine nuts enhances their flavour

1 Heat the oven to 190°C (375°F, Gas 5). Toast the pine nuts on the baking sheet until lightly browned, stirring occasionally, 5–8 minutes.

! TAKE CARE !
Toast pine nuts until evenly coloured; do not let them burn or they will be bitter.

2 Bring a medium saucepan of salted water to a boil. Add the rice and bring back to a boil. Simmer until the rice is just tender, 10–12 minutes. Stir occasionally to prevent the rice from sticking to the bottom of the pan.

3 Meanwhile, peel the onions, leaving a little of the root attached, and cut them in half through root and stem. Lay each onion half flat on the chopping board and slice horizontally towards the root, leaving the slices attached at the root end.

4 Slice vertically, again leaving the root end intact. Then cut across the onion to make dice, guiding the knife with your knuckles.

Dill and mint are classic flavouring herbs for stuffed vine leaves

5 Strip the herb leaves from the stalks, reserving a few small dill and mint sprigs for garnish, and pile them on the chopping board. With the chef's knife, coarsely chop the leaves. Squeeze the juice from the lemons; there should be 90 ml (6 tbsp) juice.

6 Drain the rice in the sieve, rinse with cold water to wash away the starch, and drain again thoroughly.

7 Heat one-third of the oil in a large saucepan. Add the onions and cook until soft but not brown, 3–5 minutes.

Stir rice stuffing well to mix ingredients before tasting for seasoning

Sultanas add hint of sweetness to stuffing

8 Stir in the rice, toasted pine nuts, sultanas, chopped herbs, one-quarter of the lemon juice, salt, and pepper. Taste for seasoning.

ANNE SAYS
"Be sure that the stuffing is highly seasoned at this stage because the flavours will mellow and become subdued during cooking."

2 STUFF THE VINE LEAVES

1 Bring a saucepan of water to a boil. Put the vine leaves in a bowl and cover with boiling water.

2 Separate the leaves with the wooden spoon. Let the leaves stand in the water 15 minutes or according to package directions.

3 Drain the leaves in the colander, rinse with cold water, and drain again thoroughly.

4 Place the vine leaves in layers between sheets of paper towels and pat gently to dry.

Blanched vine leaves are supple and will be easy to roll

Paper towels absorb excess water from vine leaves

5 Spread about 8 vine leaves over the bottom of the sauté pan to prevent the rolled and stuffed leaves from sticking to the pan.

! TAKE CARE !
The vine leaves can be torn easily, so handle them gently.

Rice stuffing is full of sultanas and pine nuts

6 Spread 1 of the remaining vine leaves flat on the work surface, vein-side up with the stem end towards you. Put 1–2 spoonfuls of the rice stuffing in the centre of the leaf.

7 Fold the sides and stem end of the leaf over the stuffing. Starting at the stem end, roll up the leaf away from you into a neat cylinder enclosing all the stuffing. Repeat with the remaining leaves and stuffing.

Vine leaves roll into neat packages

ANNE SAYS
"If the leaves are small, use 2 leaves for each roll and slightly overlap them."

3 COOK AND FINISH THE STUFFED VINE LEAVES

Use correct size pan so leaves are tightly packed in single layer

1 Pack the stuffed leaves tightly, in a single layer, in the sauté pan so they do not unroll during cooking.

Chicken stock imparts extra flavour to rolls

2 Pour the chicken stock or water over the vine leaves. Add half of the remaining oil and half of the remaining lemon juice.

ANNE SAYS
"The liquid prevents the leaves from drying out and ensures even cooking."

Pour in stock to just cover leaves

Leaves are covered with liquid throughout cooking

3 Cover the vine leaves with the heatproof plate. Bring to a boil on top of the stove, then cover the pan with the lid, and simmer over low heat, 45–60 minutes.

! TAKE CARE !
The stuffed leaves must always be covered with liquid so you may need to add more water during cooking.

4 To test when done, pierce the leaves with the skewer; they should be very tender. Let stuffed vine leaves cool in the pan.

5 Transfer the cooked leaves to the non-metallic dish. Spoon over any remaining cooking liquid, cover, and marinate in the refrigerator at least 12 hours so the flavours can mellow.

Cooking liquid keeps stuffed vine leaves moist while they marinate

🍽 TO SERVE

Set the stuffed vine leaves on a serving platter and spoon over the remaining olive oil and lemon juice. Garnish with the reserved dill and mint sprigs, plus rings of red, yellow, and green pepper, if you like.

Lemon juice and fruity olive oil give shine to stuffed vine leaves

Vine leaves enclose tasty stuffing of rice, pine nuts, sultanas, and herbs

VARIATION

LAMB-AND-RICE-STUFFED VINE LEAVES

Minced lamb and spices add substance to the filling for vine leaves here, which are served with a simple yogurt and chopped mint sauce.

1 Omit the pine nuts, fresh dill, and sultanas from the stuffing.
2 Cook 150 g (5 oz) rice as directed.
3 Sauté the chopped onions in 60 ml (4 tbsp) olive oil. Add 375 g (12 oz) minced lamb to the softened onions and cook, stirring, until it loses its pink colour, 5–7 minutes.
4 Chop the leaves from a large bunch of fresh mint.

5 Stir the rice, chopped mint, juice of $1/2$ lemon, 2.5 ml ($1/2$ tsp) ground cinnamon, a pinch of ground nutmeg, salt, and pepper into the lamb mixture.
6 Stuff the vine leaves as directed, using small leaves or cutting larger leaves lengthwise in half. Cook, using water instead of chicken stock.
7 Serve warm, with a plain yogurt and chopped mint sauce. Garnish with fresh mint, if you like.

CHICKEN LIVER AND APPLE PATE

¡O¡ SERVES 6 🥣 WORK TIME 30–35 MINUTES* 🍲 COOKING TIME 12–15 MINUTES

EQUIPMENT

125 ml (4 fl oz) ramekins

food processor†

apple corer

vegetable peeler

frying pan

small knife

bowls

chef's knife

palette knife

7.5 cm (3 inch) pastry cutter

2-pronged fork

rubber spatula

chopping board

wooden spoon

metal spoon

slotted spoon

†blender can also be used

The smooth richness of the chicken livers is pleasantly contrasted with the sweet sautéed apples. A touch of Calvados or Cognac is added and then flamed for depth of flavour. Topped with golden slices of caramelized apple, these individual pâtés make an elegant first course.

GETTING AHEAD

The chicken liver pâté can be kept up to 2 days, covered, in the refrigerator and the flavour will mellow. Prepare the decoration and add just before serving.

*plus 2–3 hours chilling time

metric	SHOPPING LIST	imperial
4	shallots	4
2	garlic cloves	2
500 g	chicken livers	1 lb
3	dessert apples	3
250 g	butter	8 oz
	salt and pepper	
60 ml	Calvados	4 tbsp
30 ml	caster sugar	2 tbsp
6	sprigs of fresh mint for decoration	6
6	slices of wholemeal bread	6

INGREDIENTS

chicken livers

shallots

Calvados†

garlic

dessert apples

wholemeal bread

butter

caster sugar

mint

†Cognac can also be used

ORDER OF WORK

1 PREPARE THE INGREDIENTS

2 MAKE THE CHICKEN LIVER PATE

3 PREPARE THE GARNISH

1 PREPARE THE INGREDIENTS

Cook apples briskly so they keep their shape

1 Peel the shallots, set flat-side down, and slice. Then chop them to make fine dice. Discard the skin from the garlic cloves and finely chop the garlic.

2 Trim any membrane from the chicken livers with the small knife. Core, peel, and dice 2 of the apples (see box, below).

3 Melt 30 ml (2 tbsp) butter in the frying pan. Add the diced apples, salt, and pepper to the pan.

HOW TO CORE, PEEL, AND DICE APPLES

If you remove an apple core with a corer, the fruit is left whole and easy to dice.

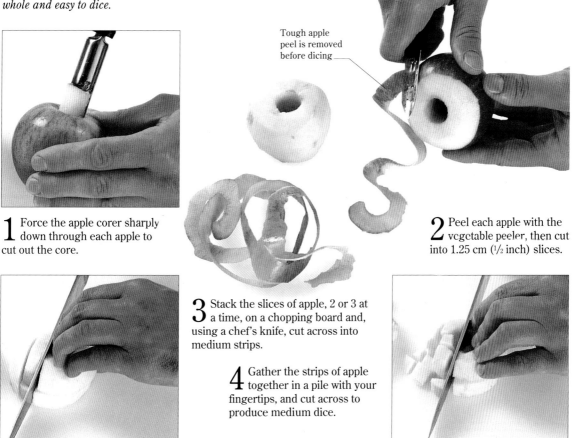

Tough apple peel is removed before dicing

1 Force the apple corer sharply down through each apple to cut out the core.

2 Peel each apple with the vegetable peeler, then cut into 1.25 cm (1/2 inch) slices.

3 Stack the slices of apple, 2 or 3 at a time, on a chopping board and, using a chef's knife, cut across into medium strips.

4 Gather the strips of apple together in a pile with your fingertips, and cut across to produce medium dice.

Diced apples add
hint of sweetness
to chicken liver
pâté

4 Sauté the apples, stirring frequently, until tender, 5–7 minutes. Transfer the diced apples to a bowl with the slotted spoon.

Apples cook in
butter until slightly
soft and golden

5 Melt another 30 ml (2 tbsp) butter in the frying pan. Add the chicken livers, salt, and pepper to the pan. Fry the livers, stirring, until brown on the outside, 2–3 minutes.

6 Scrape the chopped garlic and shallots into the frying pan.

7 Continue cooking the livers, garlic, and shallots, stirring, until the shallots are slightly softened, 1–2 minutes.

Fry livers rapidly
so they remain
pink in centre

8 Remove a liver from the frying pan, then slice into it to test whether it is cooked. It should be very brown but still pink in the centre.

9 Increase the heat to medium-high. Pour the Calvados into the pan and bring to a boil.

Crisp particles in bottom of pan are loosened by adding Calvados

Allow Calvados to boil so some alcohol cooks off before you light it

10 Hold a lighted match to the pan's side to set the alcohol alight.

! TAKE CARE !
Flames can rise quite high, so stand back from the pan. Use a long-handled spoon for basting.

11 Baste the chicken livers until the flames subside, 20–30 seconds. Let the livers cool.

2 MAKE THE CHICKEN LIVER PATE

1 Purée the chicken liver mixture in the food processor until almost smooth. Wipe out the frying pan.

ANNE SAYS
"Little bits of crusty liver from the pan add texture to the pâté."

2 With the wooden spoon or an electric mixer, cream 150 g (5 oz) butter until very soft.

3 Add the chicken liver purée with the diced and sautéed apples to the creamed butter.

4 Using the wooden spoon, mix the ingredients together thoroughly. Season the pâté to taste.

5 Spoon the mixture into six ramekins, filling them at least three-quarters full. Smooth the tops with the back of a spoon dipped in hot water so it does not stick to the pâté. Cover and chill until firm, 2–3 hours. Meanwhile, prepare the garnish.

Back of spoon dipped in hot water makes surface of pâté smooth

3 **PREPARE THE GARNISH**

1 Leaving the skin on, core the remaining apple and cut it crosswise into 6 slices. Melt the remaining butter in the frying pan. Add the apple slices, and sprinkle them with half of the sugar.

Do not allow caramel to burn or it will be bitter

Sugar forms caramel coating on apple slices

2 Turn the slices over, and sprinkle with the remaining sugar. Fry the apple slices over medium heat until they are caramelized and browned, 2–3 minutes on each side. Transfer them to a plate and reserve. Meanwhile, prepare the mint decoration and toast.

Mint sprigs bring fresh aroma and colour to finished dish

3 For the decoration, carefully remove the top mint sprigs from the stalks and reserve.

4 Toast the slices of wholemeal bread. Cut out large circles from the toast using the pastry cutter, or cut the slices into triangles, if you prefer.

🍴 TO SERVE
Set a caramelized apple slice and a mint sprig on top of each pâté and serve with the toast.

Caramelized apple echoes flavouring in pâté

CHICKEN LIVER PATE WITH ORANGE

Ramekins, small cups, moulds, or pots, about 5 cm (2 inches) deep, make ideal containers for this plain chicken liver pâté, topped with orange segments.

1 Omit the apples and sugar. Make the pâté as directed, using only 175 g (6 oz) butter and substituting Grand Marnier or Cointreau for the Calvados. Spoon the pâté into the chosen containers, then chill them.

2 Segment 1 orange for decoration: slice off the top and bottom of the orange. Cut away the peel and white pith, following the curve of the fruit. Working over a bowl, cut down each side of the orange segments to separate them from the membranes, discarding the pips as you go. Put the segments on a plate, cover, and refrigerate.

3 Just before serving, top each of the ramekins with 2 orange segments, and accompany with triangles of toasted wholemeal bread.

Wholemeal toast is a classic accompaniment to chicken liver pâté

GREEK-STYLE PIQUANT VEGETABLES

Légumes à la grecque

🍽 SERVES 6–8　🥣 WORK TIME 25–30 MINUTES　🍲 COOKING TIME 25–30 MINUTES

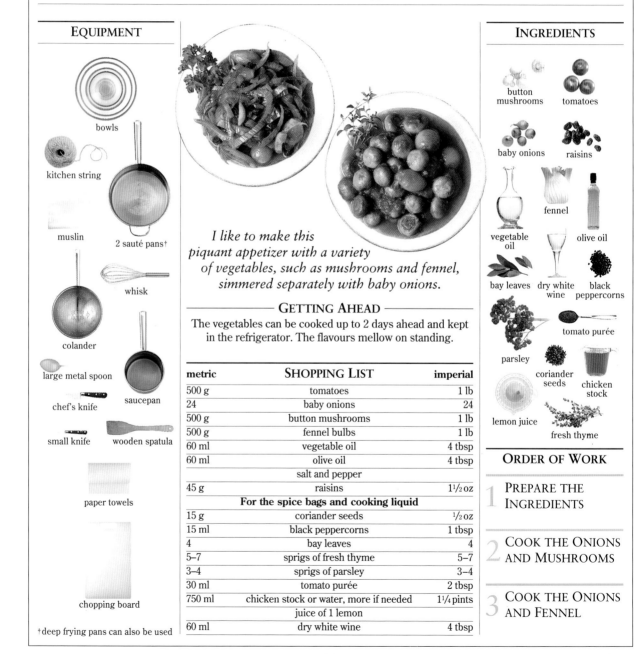

EQUIPMENT

bowls

kitchen string

muslin

2 sauté pans†

whisk

colander

large metal spoon

chef's knife

saucepan

small knife

wooden spatula

paper towels

chopping board

†deep frying pans can also be used

I like to make this piquant appetizer with a variety of vegetables, such as mushrooms and fennel, simmered separately with baby onions.

GETTING AHEAD

The vegetables can be cooked up to 2 days ahead and kept in the refrigerator. The flavours mellow on standing.

metric	SHOPPING LIST	imperial
500 g	tomatoes	1 lb
24	baby onions	24
500 g	button mushrooms	1 lb
500 g	fennel bulbs	1 lb
60 ml	vegetable oil	4 tbsp
60 ml	olive oil	4 tbsp
	salt and pepper	
45 g	raisins	1½ oz
	For the spice bags and cooking liquid	
15 g	coriander seeds	½ oz
15 ml	black peppercorns	1 tbsp
4	bay leaves	4
5–7	sprigs of fresh thyme	5–7
3–4	sprigs of parsley	3–4
30 ml	tomato purée	2 tbsp
750 ml	chicken stock or water, more if needed	1¼ pints
	juice of 1 lemon	
60 ml	dry white wine	4 tbsp

INGREDIENTS

button mushrooms

tomatoes

baby onions

raisins

vegetable oil

fennel

olive oil

bay leaves

dry white wine

black peppercorns

tomato purée

parsley

coriander seeds

chicken stock

lemon juice

fresh thyme

ORDER OF WORK

1 PREPARE THE INGREDIENTS

2 COOK THE ONIONS AND MUSHROOMS

3 COOK THE ONIONS AND FENNEL

1 PREPARE THE INGREDIENTS

Flavourings tied in
muslin will be easy
to remove when
cooking is finished

1 Combine the coriander seeds,
black peppercorns, bay leaves, thyme
sprigs, and parsley sprigs. Halve the mixture
and tie each portion up in a piece of muslin.

2 Make the cooking liquid: whisk the
tomato purée, half of the chicken
stock or water, the lemon juice, and
white wine in a bowl.

3 Core the tomatoes. Score an "x"
on the base of each. Immerse in
boiling water, 8–15 seconds. Transfer
to cold water, reserving the hot water.
When cooled, peel and cut crosswise
in half. Squeeze out the seeds, then
coarsely chop each half.

4 Put the baby onions in a
bowl, cover with the hot
water, and let stand, 2 minutes.
Drain and peel them, leaving
a little of the root attached.

6 Wash each fennel bulb; trim the
stalks and roots, discarding any
tough outer pieces from the bulbs.
Cut the fennel bulbs lengthwise in half.
Set each half cut-side down and slice.

Fennel
adds subtle
liquorice
flavour

5 Wipe the mushroom caps with
damp paper towels and trim the
stalks level with the caps. Cut the
caps into quarters if large.

2 COOK THE ONIONS AND MUSHROOMS

1 Heat half of the vegetable oil and half of the olive oil in a sauté pan. Add half of the baby onions and sauté until lightly browned, about 3 minutes.

Tomatoes will reduce down, adding colour and flavour to sauce

2 Add the mushrooms, a spice bag, and the chopped tomatoes to the sauté pan.

3 Pour in half of the cooking liquid – there should be enough to almost cover the vegetables; if necessary, add more stock or water. Add salt. Bring to a fast boil over high heat.

Use tip of knife to test vegetables for tenderness

4 Continue boiling rapidly, stirring occasionally. Add a little stock or water as the liquid evaporates, so the vegetables do not stick. Cook until the vegetables are tender when pierced with the tip of a small knife, 25–30 minutes. Meanwhile, cook the remaining onions and fennel (see below).

3 COOK THE ONIONS AND FENNEL

1 Heat the remaining vegetable oil and olive oil in the second sauté pan and sauté the rest of the baby onions until lightly browned, about 3 minutes.

2 Put the second spice bag, remaining cooking liquid, and salt in the pan. Add the sliced fennel and bring the liquid to a fast boil over high heat.

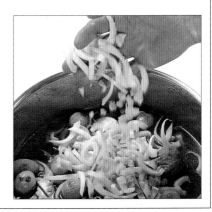

3 Continue boiling, 10–12 minutes, then add the raisins to the fennel and onions in the sauté pan, and stir together to combine.

4 Continue boiling rapidly, stirring occasionally, and adding a little stock or water as the liquid evaporates. Cook until the onions and fennel are tender when pierced with the tip of a knife, 15–20 minutes. Remove the spice bags from both mixtures and taste for seasoning.

As cooking liquid reduces flavours are concentrated

🍽 TO SERVE
Serve the vegetable mixtures in separate bowls at room temperature. Decorate the fennel with a sprig of parsley and the mushrooms with a sprig of fresh thyme, if you like.

Piquant vegetables are served in glass bowls so that rich colours can be appreciated

Cooking liquid is aromatic with coriander, peppercorns, bay leaf, parsley, and thyme

GOLDEN GREEK-STYLE VEGETABLES

1 Omit the mushrooms, fennel, and raisins. Make the spice bags as directed, using 20 g (³/₄ oz) coriander seeds, 22.5 ml (1¹/₂ tbsp) peppercorns, 4 bay leaves, 9–12 sprigs of fresh coriander, and 6–9 sprigs of parsley.
2 Prepare the cooking liquid, the tomatoes, and onions as directed. Trim the florets from 1 small cauliflower (weighing about 750 g/1¹/₂ lb), cutting them in half if large. Wash and trim 2 courgettes (total weight about 500 g/1 lb) and cut them into 5 mm (¹/₄ inch) slices. Soak a large pinch of saffron in a little boiling water.
3 Heat 30 ml (2 tbsp) each vegetable oil and olive oil in each of 2 sauté pans. Divide the baby onions between the 2 pans. Add the cauliflower, a spice bag, half of the cooking liquid, half of the saffron with its liquid, and salt to 1 pan.
4 Put the courgettes in the other pan with a spice bag, the tomatoes, the remaining cooking liquid, saffron with its liquid, and salt.
5 Cook until tender, 25–30 minutes, adding more stock or water as necessary.
6 Serve in separate bowls, decorating the courgettes with coriander leaves, and the cauliflower with a bay leaf, if you like.

SMOKED TROUT MOUSSE WITH HORSERADISH AND DILL

🍴 SERVES 8–10 🥄 WORK TIME 20–25 MINUTES*

EQUIPMENT

1.25 litre (2 pint) terrine mould with lid

chef's knife

bowls

small knife

rubber spatula

whisk†

pastry brush

small saucepan

chopping board

† electric mixer can also be used

ANNE SAYS

"If using a mould made from aluminium or tin, do not store the mousse in it longer than 4 hours, or it will discolour the mousse and taint the flavour."

Made with flaked, smoked trout in a mayonnaise base lightened with yogurt, this mousse is a refreshing start to any meal. I sometimes use a fish-shaped mould for a more festive presentation.

— GETTING AHEAD —
The mousse can be prepared up to 1 day ahead and kept, covered, in the refrigerator.

*plus 3–4 hours chilling time

metric	SHOPPING LIST	imperial
2	eggs	2
3	small spring onions	3
1	small bunch of fresh dill	1
2	smoked trout, total weight about 750 g (1½ lb)	2
	vegetable oil for mould	
15 ml	powdered gelatine	1 tbsp
60 ml	cold water	4 tbsp
125 ml	bottled mayonnaise	4 fl oz
125 ml	plain yogurt	4 fl oz
60 g	grated fresh horseradish, more to taste	2 oz
	juice of 1 lemon	
	salt and pepper	
175 ml	double cream	6 fl oz
1	bunch of watercress for serving	1

INGREDIENTS

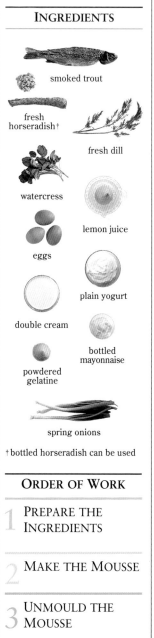

smoked trout

fresh horseradish†

fresh dill

watercress

lemon juice

eggs

plain yogurt

double cream

bottled mayonnaise

powdered gelatine

spring onions

† bottled horseradish can be used

ORDER OF WORK

1 PREPARE THE INGREDIENTS

2 MAKE THE MOUSSE

3 UNMOULD THE MOUSSE

1 PREPARE THE INGREDIENTS

1 Put the eggs in the sauccpan, cover with cold water, and bring to a boil. Simmer 10 minutes. Drain the eggs; let them cool in a bowl of cold water. Tap the eggs to crack the shells, peel them, and rinse with cold water. Coarsely chop the eggs.

Egg adds texture to mousse

Egg should be coarsely chopped

Hold egg with your fingertips as you chop

2 Trim the spring onions and finely slice them, including the trimmed green tops.

4 Remove the skin from the smoked trout by peeling it off with the help of the small knife. Then carefully lift off the fish fillets from the bones; discard the heads, bones, and skin.

Skin separates easily from flesh of smoked trout

3 Strip the dill leaves from the stalks and pile them on the chopping board. With the chef's knife, finely chop the leaves.

5 Holding the fillets in 1 hand, flake the trout flesh with a fork. Brush the mould with oil.

6 Sprinkle the gelatine over the cold water in a small bowl and let stand until the granules become spongy, about 5 minutes.

BLINI WITH SMOKED SALMON

🍴 SERVES 8 🥣 WORK TIME 25–30 MINUTES* 🍲 COOKING TIME 8–16 MINUTES

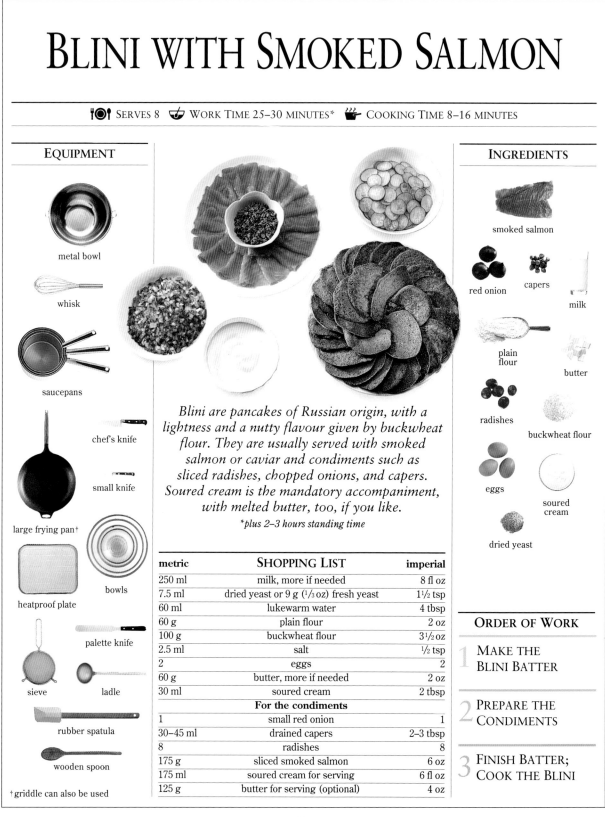

EQUIPMENT

metal bowl

whisk

saucepans

chef's knife

small knife

large frying pan†

heatproof plate

bowls

palette knife

sieve

ladle

rubber spatula

wooden spoon

†griddle can also be used

INGREDIENTS

smoked salmon

red onion

capers

milk

plain flour

butter

radishes

buckwheat flour

eggs

soured cream

dried yeast

Blini are pancakes of Russian origin, with a lightness and a nutty flavour given by buckwheat flour. They are usually served with smoked salmon or caviar and condiments such as sliced radishes, chopped onions, and capers. Soured cream is the mandatory accompaniment, with melted butter, too, if you like.

*plus 2–3 hours standing time

metric	SHOPPING LIST	imperial
250 ml	milk, more if needed	8 fl oz
7.5 ml	dried yeast or 9 g (¹/₃ oz) fresh yeast	1¹/₂ tsp
60 ml	lukewarm water	4 tbsp
60 g	plain flour	2 oz
100 g	buckwheat flour	3¹/₂ oz
2.5 ml	salt	¹/₂ tsp
2	eggs	2
60 g	butter, more if needed	2 oz
30 ml	soured cream	2 tbsp
	For the condiments	
1	small red onion	1
30–45 ml	drained capers	2–3 tbsp
8	radishes	8
175 g	sliced smoked salmon	6 oz
175 ml	soured cream for serving	6 fl oz
125 g	butter for serving (optional)	4 oz

ORDER OF WORK

1 MAKE THE BLINI BATTER

2 PREPARE THE CONDIMENTS

3 FINISH BATTER; COOK THE BLINI

1 MAKE THE BLINI BATTER

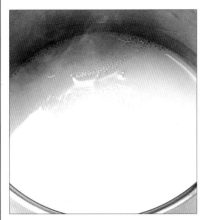

1 Pour three-quarters of the milk into a saucepan and bring just to a boil over medium heat. Let the milk cool to lukewarm.

2 Meanwhile, sprinkle or crumble the yeast over the lukewarm water in a small bowl and let stand until dissolved, about 5 minutes.

3 Sift the plain flour with the buckwheat flour and salt into a large bowl. Using your fingers, make a well in the centre.

4 Add the yeast mixture and the lukewarm milk to the well.

5 Stir the mixture with the wooden spoon, gradually drawing the flour into the centre. Beat the mixture well to make a smooth batter, about 2 minutes. Dampen a tea towel and cover the bowl. Transfer to a warm place and let the batter rise until it is light and full of bubbles, 2–3 hours, as illustrated bottom right. While the batter is rising, prepare the condiments (see page 44).

Batter with buckwheat flour is shiny and slightly glutinous in texture

Wooden spoon blends batter evenly

2 PREPARE THE CONDIMENTS

1 Peel the red onion, leaving the root attached, and cut it in half. Slice each half horizontally towards the root, but not through it.

2 Slice the onion vertically, again leaving the root end uncut. Finally, cut across the onion to make dice. Continue chopping the onion until it is very fine. Put the chopped onion in a small bowl.

3 Coarsely chop the drained capers if they are large. Transfer them to a small serving bowl.

Leave some root to hold onion layers together

Discard papery onion skins

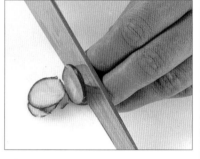

4 Trim the roots and tops from the radishes. Wash, dry, then thinly slice the radishes.

Fold smoked salmon slices for attractive presentation

5 Put the sliced radishes in a small serving bowl. Cover the radishes, onions, and capers, and set aside until ready to serve.

6 Arrange the slices of smoked salmon on a serving plate, cover and keep in the refrigerator.

3 FINISH BATTER; COOK THE BLINI

1 Heat the oven to low for keeping the blini warm. Separate the eggs. Melt half of the butter in a small saucepan and cool slightly. Pour the remaining milk into the risen batter and stir until mixed.

2 Stir in the egg yolks, melted butter, and soured cream. Add more milk if necessary so the batter is the consistency of double cream.

Egg yolks enrich batter

For stiff texture, always use a metal bowl when whisking egg whites

3 Put the egg whites into the metal bowl and beat with the whisk until stiff peaks form when the whisk is lifted, 3–5 minutes.

! TAKE CARE !
Do not overbeat the egg whites or they will become grainy.

4 Add about one-quarter of the beaten egg whites to the blini batter and gently stir with the rubber spatula until thoroughly mixed.

Rubber spatula makes folding easy by cutting through egg whites and batter

5 Pour the batter and egg-white mixture into the metal bowl with the remaining beaten egg whites.

6 Fold the mixture together: cut down into the centre of the bowl with the rubber spatula, scoop under the contents and turn them over in a rolling motion. At the same time, with your other hand, turn the bowl anti-clockwise. Continue folding until the batter is thoroughly blended.

7 Heat half of the remaining butter in the frying pan. Ladle in the batter to make 7.5 cm (3 inch) rounds.

ANNE SAYS
"Do not overcrowd the blini in the pan."

Small bubbles appear on surface

Batter will spread slightly on hot frying pan

8 Cook until the underside of the blini are lightly browned and the tops are bubbling, 1–2 minutes. Turn them over and brown the other side.

9 Transfer the blini to the heatproof plate, overlapping them so they remain moist, and keep warm in the heated oven. Continue to make blini, adding more butter to the pan as needed.

Smoked salmon is a colourful and tasty accompaniment to blini

🍽 TO SERVE

Melt the butter, if using. Arrange the blini on a serving plate and serve, accompanied by the chopped onions, capers, radish slices, and smoked salmon. Serve a bowl of soured cream separately, and a bowl of melted butter if you like.

Chopped sweet red onion complements nutty flavour of blini

VARIATION

BLINI WITH RED AND BLACK CAVIAR

Choose lumpfish or beluga sturgeon caviar, depending on your budget.

1 Make the blini batter as directed. Omit the red onion, capers, radishes, and smoked salmon.
2 Hard-boil 2 eggs. Peel the eggs then separate the yolks and whites; finely chop them both. Trim 2 spring onions and cut the green tops into thin diagonal slices. Finish the batter and cook the blini as directed. Serve them with 30 g (1 oz) each red and black caviar (or more to taste), egg yolks and whites, spring onion slices, and a spoonful of soured cream.

GETTING AHEAD

The bowls of condiments can be prepared up to 2–3 hours ahead and kept tightly covered. The blini are best cooked at the last minute, although they can be made up to 8 hours ahead and warmed in a low oven just before serving.

MARINATED GOAT CHEESE SALAD

Salade de Chèvre Mariné

🍽 SERVES 8   🥣 WORK TIME 20–25 MINUTES*   🍲 COOKING TIME 5–8 MINUTES

EQUIPMENT

large glass jar with lid†

slotted spoon

whisk

pastry brush

colander

small knife

palette knife

sieve

bowl

salad bowl

paper towels

7.5 cm (3 inch) pastry cutter

baking sheet

†shallow non-metallic bowl and cling film can also be used

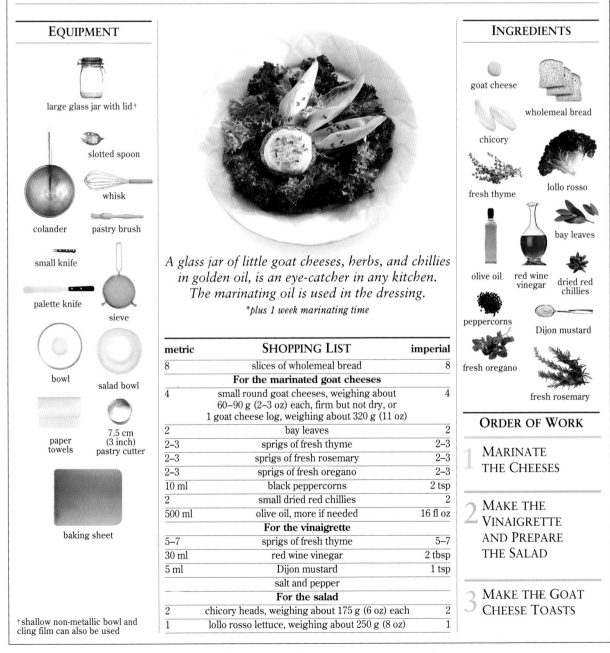

A glass jar of little goat cheeses, herbs, and chillies in golden oil, is an eye-catcher in any kitchen. The marinating oil is used in the dressing.

*plus 1 week marinating time

INGREDIENTS

goat cheese

wholemeal bread

chicory

lollo rosso

fresh thyme

bay leaves

olive oil   red wine vinegar   dried red chillies

peppercorns

Dijon mustard

fresh oregano

fresh rosemary

SHOPPING LIST

metric	SHOPPING LIST	imperial
8	slices of wholemeal bread	8
	For the marinated goat cheeses	
4	small round goat cheeses, weighing about 60–90 g (2–3 oz) each, firm but not dry, or 1 goat cheese log, weighing about 320 g (11 oz)	4
2	bay leaves	2
2–3	sprigs of fresh thyme	2–3
2–3	sprigs of fresh rosemary	2–3
2–3	sprigs of fresh oregano	2–3
10 ml	black peppercorns	2 tsp
2	small dried red chillies	2
500 ml	olive oil, more if needed	16 fl oz
	For the vinaigrette	
5–7	sprigs of fresh thyme	5–7
30 ml	red wine vinegar	2 tbsp
5 ml	Dijon mustard	1 tsp
	salt and pepper	
	For the salad	
2	chicory heads, weighing about 175 g (6 oz) each	2
1	lollo rosso lettuce, weighing about 250 g (8 oz)	1

ORDER OF WORK

1 MARINATE THE CHEESES

2 MAKE THE VINAIGRETTE AND PREPARE THE SALAD

3 MAKE THE GOAT CHEESE TOASTS

1 MARINATE THE CHEESES

1 Put the goat cheeses in the large glass jar with the bay leaves, the 2–3 sprigs of thyme, rosemary, and oregano, the peppercorns, and chillies. Add enough olive oil to cover generously.

2 Cover the jar with its lid and leave the goat cheeses at least 1 week before using.

ANNE SAYS
"If using a goat cheese log, put it in a non-metallic bowl with the other ingredients, cover with cling film, and marinate 1–3 days only."

Fragrant herbs add flavour to olive oil marinade

2 MAKE THE VINAIGRETTE AND PREPARE THE SALAD

1 Remove the goat cheeses from the marinade with the slotted spoon, draining off any excess oil.

Oil from marinating cheeses adds depth of flavour to vinaigrette

2 Strain the oil. You will need 90 ml (3 fl oz) for the vinaigrette and a little more for the bread.

ANNE SAYS
"Any remaining oil can be kept and used for other dressings."

3 Strip the leaves from the 5–7 thyme sprigs. Whisk the vinegar in the bowl with the mustard, salt, and pepper. Gradually whisk in the reserved oil so the vinaigrette emulsifies and thickens slightly.

4 Stir in half of the thyme. Taste for seasoning and adjust if necessary.

5 Wipe the chicory with a damp paper towel, trim the stems, and discard any discoloured leaves. Separate the remaining leaves.

6 Carefully wash the lollo rosso lettuce under cold running water, discarding the tough stems, and drain the leaves well in the colander.

7 Put the chicory leaves in the salad bowl and tear the lettuce leaves into pieces as you add them; toss gently with your hands.

3 MAKE THE GOAT CHEESE TOASTS

2 Using the pastry cutter, cut out a round from each slice of wholemeal bread.

1 Heat the oven to 200°C (400°F, Gas 6). Cut each goat cheese in half horizontally.

ANNE SAYS
"If using a goat cheese log, cut it into 8 equal slices."

Trimmings can be made into breadcrumbs for future use

3 Set the bread rounds on the baking sheet and brush with a little of the strained olive oil. Bake in the heated oven until lightly toasted, 3–5 minutes.

Rounds should be slightly larger in diameter than cheese

Cheese will melt and
spread over bread

4 Heat the grill. Put
a piece of cheese
on top of each toasted
bread round. Grill until
the cheese is bubbling and
golden, 2–3 minutes.

🍴 TO SERVE

Toss the salad greens with the
vinaigrette and arrange the salad on
individual plates. Place the cheese
toasts on the salads and sprinkle
with the remaining thyme.
Serve immediately.

Fresh thyme
tastes good with
goat cheese

**Hot cheese
toasts** contrast
with cool crisp salad

V A R I A T I O N

BREADED MARINATED GOAT CHEESE SALAD

1 Marinate the goat cheeses as
directed in the main recipe.
2 Make the vinaigrette as directed.
3 Omit the chicory. Trim the stalks
from 1 bunch of watercress, wash, and
drain. Prepare 1 lollo rosso lettuce and
combine with the watercress.
4 Put 45 g (1½ oz) flour on a sheet of
greaseproof paper. Lightly beat 1 egg
and 1 large pinch of salt in a shallow
bowl. Put 60 g (2 oz) dried breadcrumbs on another sheet of paper. Coat
the marinated goat cheese halves with
flour, then dip them in the beaten egg,
and finally coat with the breadcrumbs.
Use 2 forks to turn the cheeses.
5 Heat 15 g (½ oz) butter in a frying
pan with 15 ml (1 tbsp) oil from the
marinade and sauté the cheese slices,
in 2 batches, until lightly browned and
crisp, 1–2 minutes on each side. Add
15 g (½ oz) more butter and 15 ml
(1 tbsp) more oil to the frying pan for
the second batch.
6 Toss the salad with the vinaigrette
and pile on individual plates. Serve
the hot cheese on the side.

GETTING AHEAD

Individual goat cheeses can be marinated
3–4 weeks in the refrigerator, but will soften
if kept too long. Do not marinate softer goat
cheese logs more than 3 days. Make the
cheese toasts and assemble the salad
just before serving.

SPRING ROLLS WITH LETTUCE AND MINT LEAVES

🍽 SERVES 8   🥄 WORK TIME 40–45 MINUTES*   ♨ COOKING TIME 15–25 MINUTES

EQUIPMENT

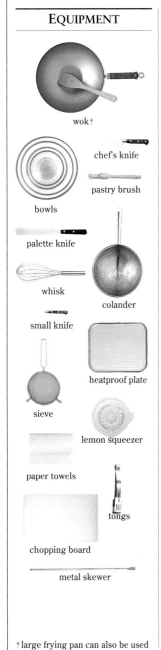

wok†

chef's knife

pastry brush

bowls

palette knife

whisk

colander

small knife

heatproof plate

sieve

lemon squeezer

paper towels

tongs

chopping board

metal skewer

†large frying pan can also be used

A wrapping of crisp iceberg lettuce and mint leaves, added by guests at the table, wonderfully lightens the oriental treat of fried spring rolls.
*plus 30 minutes soaking time

INGREDIENTS

iceberg lettuce

fresh mint

spring roll wrappers

cellophane noodles

vegetable oil

garlic cloves

minced pork

limes

honey

fish sauce

dried shiitake mushrooms

egg

crushed chillies

sugar

onion

ANNE SAYS
"Egg roll wrappers are thicker than spring roll wrappers and easier to use."

ORDER OF WORK

1   MAKE THE FILLING

2   ASSEMBLE ROLLS

3   PREPARE LETTUCE; MAKE THE SAUCE

4   FRY THE ROLLS

metric	SHOPPING LIST	imperial
16	spring or egg roll wrappers, defrosted if frozen	16
1	egg	1
1	medium head of iceberg lettuce	1
125 ml	vegetable oil for frying, more if needed	4 fl oz
1	medium bunch of fresh mint	1
	For the filling	
30 g	dried shiitake or other oriental mushrooms	1 oz
60 g	cellophane noodles	2 oz
1	medium onion	1
2	garlic cloves	2
30 ml	vegetable oil	2 tbsp
250 g	minced pork	8 oz
45 ml	Asian fish sauce (nam pla or patis)	3 tbsp
5 ml	granulated sugar	1 tsp
	ground black pepper	
	For the chilli dipping sauce	
6	garlic cloves	6
2	limes	2
250 ml	water	8 fl oz
125 ml	Asian fish sauce	4 fl oz
1	pinch of crushed chillies	1
60 ml	honey	4 tbsp

MAKE THE FILLING

1 Soak the dried mushrooms in a bowl of warm water until plump, about 30 minutes. Meanwhile, soak the cellophane noodles in a second bowl of warm water until softened, about 15 minutes.

Dried mushrooms have robust flavour

Warm water softens brittle cellophane noodles

2 Drain the noodles and cut them across into about 5 cm (2 inch) lengths. Drain the mushrooms and finely chop them.

ANNE SAYS
"Once the noodles are soaked they are easily cut into pieces."

3 Peel the onion, leaving a little of the root attached, and cut it lengthwise in half. Slice each half horizontally, leaving the slices attached at the root end, then slice vertically.

4 Finally, cut across the onion to make dice. Continue chopping the onion until it is fine.

Stir garlic constantly so it browns evenly

Garlic becomes fragrant as it cooks

5 Set the flat side of the chef's knife on top of each garlic clove and strike it with your fist. Discard the skin and finely chop the garlic.

6 Heat the oil in the wok, add the garlic, and cook, stirring, until fragrant, 30 seconds.

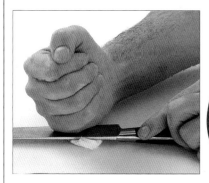

Keep stirring
to combine
ingredients and
prevent sticking

7 Add the chopped onion to the wok and continue stir-frying until softened, 1–2 minutes.

8 Add the pork and cook, stirring, until brown, 3–5 minutes. Stir in the mushrooms, cellophane noodles, fish sauce, sugar, and black pepper, and taste for seasoning.

Cellophane
noodles are soft
enough to blend
with pork and
mushrooms

2 ASSEMBLE ROLLS

Push filling onto
wrapper with
fingertip

1 Lay a damp tea towel on the work surface. Set the spring roll wrappers on half of the towel and fold the other half on top to keep them moist. Lightly beat the egg.

ANNE SAYS
"*Egg roll wrappers do not need to be kept moist. Simply spread them on the work surface.*"

Arrange filling
on wrapper so it
forms neat cylinder
when rolled

2 Set a wrapper on the work surface with a corner facing towards you. If using spring roll wrappers, replace the damp tea towel on top of the remaining wrappers. Put 1–2 spoonfuls of filling on the lower half of the wrapper.

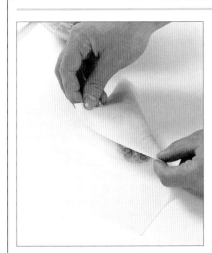

3 Fold the bottom corner of the wrapper up and over the filling.

Spring roll wrappers tear easily so handle carefully

4 Using the pastry brush or your finger, moisten the side corners with beaten egg. Fold the sides over to cover the bottom corner and the filling, and press firmly to seal.

5 Brush the top open corner of the wrapper with a little of the beaten egg to seal the spring roll.

6 Hold the wrapper steady with both hands and roll it up into a cylinder shape.

Beaten egg holds spring roll wrapper together

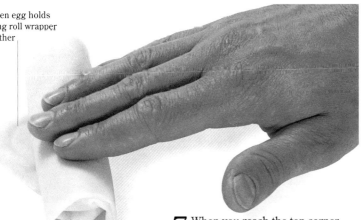

7 When you reach the top corner, press gently to seal. Transfer the spring roll to the plate.

8 Repeat with the remaining wrappers and filling, placing the sealed rolls on a plate; set aside.

3 PREPARE LETTUCE; MAKE THE SAUCE

1 Cut the core from the lettuce with the small knife. Hold the lettuce, core upwards, under cold running water, so the force of the water separates the leaves. There should be at least 16 leaves. Wash the leaves and shake them dry.

Cut deeply into iceberg lettuce to remove entire core

Hold lettuce firmly while cutting out core

2 Wrap the lettuce in damp paper towels and keep in the refrigerator while you are frying the spring rolls.

3 Peel and finely chop the garlic. Squeeze the limes. There should be 75 ml (2½ fl oz) juice. Combine the garlic, lime juice, water, fish sauce, and crushed chillies. Add the honey.

4 FRY THE ROLLS

2 During frying, turn the spring rolls until they are evenly browned and the filling is warm.

Tongs grasp spring rolls for easy turning

1 Heat the oven to low to keep spring rolls warm. Heat the vegetable oil in the wok. Fry the spring rolls in batches, 3–5 minutes. Add more oil, if necessary, between batches.

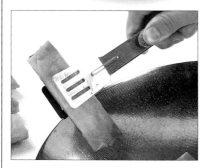

Skewer tests if spring rolls are done

Batch of 3 spring rolls fits neatly in wok

3 To test that the filling is cooked, insert the skewer in a roll. The skewer should feel warm when withdrawn after 30 seconds.

4 Transfer the spring rolls to the heatproof plate lined with paper towels to drain. Keep warm in the oven.

🍽 TO SERVE

Arrange lettuce leaves and mint leaves on each individual plate. Divide the spring rolls among the plates. Serve with a small bowl of sweet-sour sauce for dipping.

To eat a spring roll, wrap it in a lettuce leaf with 1–2 mint leaves and dip it in sauce

SPRING ROLLS FILLED WITH PRAWNS

1 Omit the lettuce and mint from the main recipe. Make a carrot salad: shred 6 peeled carrots in a food processor or on a hand grater. In a bowl, combine 125 ml (4 fl oz) water, 15 ml (1 tbsp) cider vinegar, 15 ml (1 tbsp) granulated sugar, and 2.5 ml ($^{1}/_{2}$ tsp) salt; add the carrots. Let stand at least 1 hour to marinate.

2 Meanwhile, make the filling: prepare the mushrooms, cellophane noodles, onion, and garlic as directed. Omit the pork. Chop 250 g (8 oz) peeled cooked prawns. With a small knife, peel the skin from 1.25 cm ($^{1}/_{2}$ inch) piece of fresh root ginger. With a chef's knife, slice the ginger, cutting across the fibrous grain. Crush each slice with the flat of the knife, then finely chop.

3 Heat the garlic and ginger in the oil. Add the onion and stir-fry until softened, 1–2 minutes. Add the prawns and stir-fry about 30 seconds. Add the other filling ingredients as directed.

4 Make the chilli sauce as directed.

5 Assemble and fry the spring rolls as directed. Serve them with the sauce, and the well-drained carrot salad.

GETTING AHEAD

The dipping sauce can be made up to 8 hours ahead and kept refrigerated; add the crushed chillies not more than 1 hour before serving so the sauce is not too hot. The spring rolls can be assembled up to 8 hours ahead and kept, covered, in the refrigerator. Fry them just before serving.

STUFFED MUSHROOMS WITH HERBS

¶❶¶ SERVES 4 ⟡ WORK TIME 25–30 MINUTES ♨ BAKING TIME 15–20 MINUTES

EQUIPMENT

chef's knife

pastry brush

small knife

frying pan

wooden spoon

cheese grater

paper towels

medium baking dish

bowls

chopping board

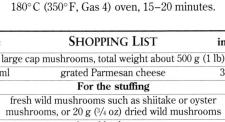

Stuffed mushrooms are hard to beat. These are filled with chopped wild mushrooms and walnuts, perfumed with garlic and plenty of herbs.

GETTING AHEAD
The mushrooms can be stuffed up to 4 hours ahead and kept, covered, in the refrigerator. Bake them, in a 180°C (350°F, Gas 4) oven, 15–20 minutes.

metric	SHOPPING LIST	imperial
12	large cap mushrooms, total weight about 500 g (1 lb)	12
45–60 ml	grated Parmesan cheese	3–4 tbsp
	For the stuffing	
90 g	fresh wild mushrooms such as shiitake or oyster mushrooms, or 20 g (³/₄ oz) dried wild mushrooms	3 oz
12–14	sprigs of fresh tarragon	12–14
10–12	sprigs of fresh chervil	10–12
7–10	sprigs of fresh thyme	7–10
100 g	walnut halves or pieces	3¹/₂ oz
3	garlic cloves	3
60 ml	olive oil, more for baking dish	4 tbsp
	juice of ¹/₂ lemon	
	salt and pepper	
90 ml	double cream	3 fl oz

INGREDIENTS

large cap mushrooms

fresh wild mushrooms

fresh tarragon

fresh chervil†

fresh thyme

lemon juice

Parmesan cheese

garlic cloves

olive oil

walnuts

double cream

† parsley can also be used

ORDER OF WORK

1 **PREPARE THE MUSHROOMS AND STUFFING**

2 **STUFF AND BAKE THE MUSHROOMS**

1 PREPARE THE MUSHROOMS AND STUFFING

1 Pull out the stalks from the large mushrooms, leaving the caps whole for stuffing. Wipe the caps with damp paper towels. Trim the stalks.

Remove stalks carefully so caps do not break

Mushroom caps are ideal containers for stuffing

2 Wipe the fresh wild mushrooms and trim the stalks. If using dried mushrooms, soak them in hot water until plump, about 30 minutes. Drain them and cut into pieces.

3 Slice the wild mushrooms and large mushroom stalks, then stack the slices, and cut across to make dice. Finely chop the dice. Alternatively, chop the mushrooms in a food processor, taking care not to overwork them or they will form a purée.

Tarragon, chervil, and thyme flavour mushroom stuffing

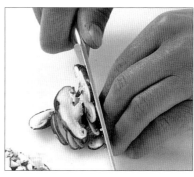

4 Set aside 4 sprigs of each herb for garnish. Chop the remaining herbs (see box, right). Combine one-quarter of the chopped herbs with the Parmesan cheese and set aside for the topping.

HOW TO CHOP FRESH HERBS

Tarragon, rosemary, chervil, parsley, dill, basil, chives, thyme, and basil are herbs that are usually chopped before being combined with other ingredients. Delicate herbs such as basil bruise easily; do not chop them too finely.

Leaves are pulled from woody stems

1 Strip the leaves or sprigs from the stalks. Pile the leaves or sprigs on a chopping board.

2 Cut the leaves or sprigs into small pieces with a chef's knife. Holding the tip of the blade against the board and rocking the blade back and forth, continue chopping the herbs.

ANNE SAYS
"When using a large quantity of herbs, or sprigs of herbs, hold them in a bunch while chopping."

5 Coarsely chop the walnuts. Set the flat side of the chef's knife on top of each garlic clove and strike it with your fist. Discard the skin and finely chop the garlic.

Herb trio lends distinctive flavour

Walnuts add crunchy texture to stuffing

6 Heat half of the oil in the frying pan. Add the chopped mushrooms and garlic with the lemon juice, salt, and pepper. Cook, stirring, until all the liquid has evaporated, 3–5 minutes. Stir in the double cream and cook until slightly thickened, 1–2 minutes. Add the walnuts and chopped herbs and stir to mix. Taste for seasoning.

STUFF AND BAKE THE MUSHROOMS

Mound stuffing in mushrooms because it will shrink slightly during baking

Seasoned mushroom caps are ready for tasty stuffing

1 Heat the oven to 180°C (350°F, Gas 4). Lightly oil the baking dish. Season the mushroom caps with salt and pepper. Spoon 1–2 spoonfuls stuffing into each mushroom cap, mounding it well. Set the stuffed mushrooms in the prepared baking dish.

MUSHROOMS STUFFED WITH SUN-DRIED TOMATOES AND CHEESE

Savoury sun-dried tomatoes are combined with two different cheeses in this stuffing.

2 Sprinkle about 5 ml (1 tsp) Parmesan and herb topping on each mushroom. Spoon the remaining oil evenly over the mushrooms. Bake in the heated oven until the mushroom caps are tender when pierced with a knife and the filling is very hot, 15–20 minutes.

Grated Parmesan will brown attractively when stuffed mushrooms are baked

¶◎¶ TO SERVE

Serve the mushrooms on a platter or on individual plates. Garnish with the reserved herbs, and additional walnuts, if you like.

1 Omit the wild mushroom and herb stuffing; chop only 3–5 sprigs each of fresh tarragon and chervil or parsley.
2 Prepare the large cap mushrooms as directed; discard the stalks.
3 Cut 60 g (2 oz) mozzarella cheese into medium dice.
4 Drain 60 ml (4 tbsp) oil-soaked sun-dried tomatoes and put them in a food processor with 4 peeled garlic cloves and 175 g (6 oz) creamy ricotta cheese. Work the ingredients to a purée. Alternatively, chop the sun-dried tomatoes and garlic finely by hand with a chef's knife, then combine them with the cheese.
5 Transfer the mixture to a bowl and stir in the chopped herbs and diced mozzarella. Season the stuffing to taste with salt and pepper.
6 Stuff the mushrooms with the tomato-cheese mixture. Sprinkle with 30 g (1 oz) grated Parmesan cheese, dividing it equally among the mushrooms. Sprinkle with oil and bake as directed.

Stuffing with wild mushrooms and crunchy walnuts is enhanced by cheese and herb topping

CHEESE PUFFS WITH SPINACH AND SMOKED SALMON

Gougères Farcies

🍽 SERVES 8 🥄 WORK TIME 40–45 MINUTES ♨ BAKING TIME 30–35 MINUTES

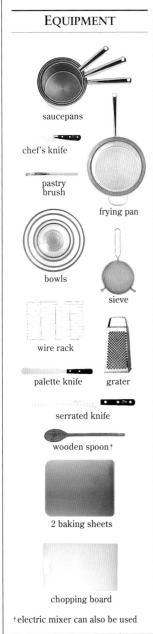

saucepans

chef's knife

pastry
brush

frying pan

bowls

sieve

wire rack

palette knife   grater

serrated knife

wooden spoon†

2 baking sheets

chopping board

†electric mixer can also be used

*Cheese puffs are traditional in Burgundy,
where they are displayed in almost every bakery
window. Here, they are filled with spinach and
smoked salmon for a modern touch.
Needless to say, a glass of white Burgundy
wine is the perfect accompaniment.*

metric	SHOPPING LIST	imperial
	For the choux pastry	
150 g	plain flour	5 oz
75 g	unsalted butter, more for baking sheets	2¾ oz
125 g	Gruyère cheese	4 oz
250 ml	water	8 fl oz
6.25 ml	salt	1¼ tsp
5–6	eggs	5–6
	For the spinach and smoked salmon filling	
1	medium onion	1
4	garlic cloves	4
1 kg	fresh spinach	2 lb
175 g	smoked salmon	6 oz
250 g	cream cheese	8 oz
30 g	butter	1 oz
1	pinch of ground nutmeg	1
	salt and pepper	
60 ml	milk	4 tbsp

INGREDIENTS

smoked salmon

fresh
spinach†   cream cheese

milk

onion

garlic cloves

butter   ground
nutmeg

eggs   Gruyère cheese

plain flour

†defrosted spinach can also be used

ORDER OF WORK

1 MAKE THE CHOUX
PASTRY DOUGH

2 GLAZE AND BAKE
THE CHEESE PUFFS

3 MAKE THE
FILLING; FILL
THE PUFFS

1 MAKE THE CHOUX PASTRY DOUGH

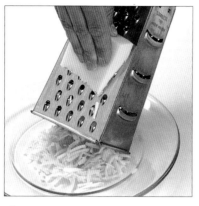

1 Sift the flour into a medium bowl. Melt a little butter and brush it over both of the baking sheets. Heat the oven to 190°C (375°F, Gas 5).

2 Using the coarse side of the grater, grate the Gruyère cheese onto a plate and set aside. Cut the butter into small pieces.

3 Melt the butter in a medium saucepan with the water and 3.75 ml (³/₄ tsp) salt. Bring just to a boil.

! TAKE CARE !
The butter must melt before the water boils or the evaporation will change the dough proportions.

Add flour to melted butter mixture all at once

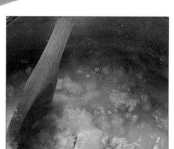

Wooden spoon is excellent to beat mixture and smooth out any lumps

4 Remove the pan from the heat and add the flour all at once. Beat the flour into the butter mixture vigorously with the wooden spoon.

5 Continue to beat until the mixture is smooth and pulls away from the side of the pan forming a ball of dough, about 1 minute. Return the pan to the stove and beat over very low heat to dry out the dough, about 30 seconds.

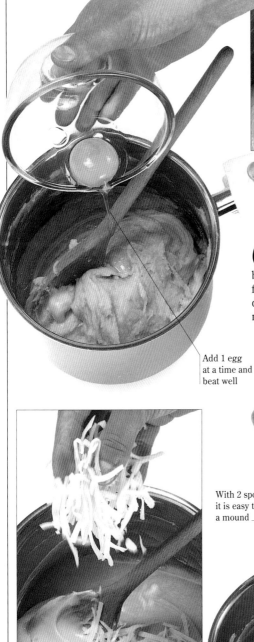

Add 1 egg
at a time and
beat well

6 Remove from the heat. Add 4 of the eggs, one at a time, beating well after each. Beat the fifth egg; add gradually until the dough is shiny and soft. You may not need all of the egg.

7 Check whether sufficient egg has been added by lifting some of the dough on the wooden spoon held over the saucepan. The dough should fall off the spoon by a count of three.

With 2 spoons
it is easy to shape
a mound

Cheese pastry dough
will be sticky but firm
enough to hold
its shape

8 Add half of the grated Gruyère cheese to the dough and stir it in until thoroughly mixed.

9 Using 2 spoons, drop eight 6 cm (2½ inch) mounds of dough on the baking sheets, leaving room for the dough to puff as it bakes.

GLAZE AND BAKE THE CHEESE PUFFS

1 Make the egg glaze: lightly beat the remaining egg with the remaining 2.5 ml (½ tsp) salt. Brush some glaze over each of the choux puffs.

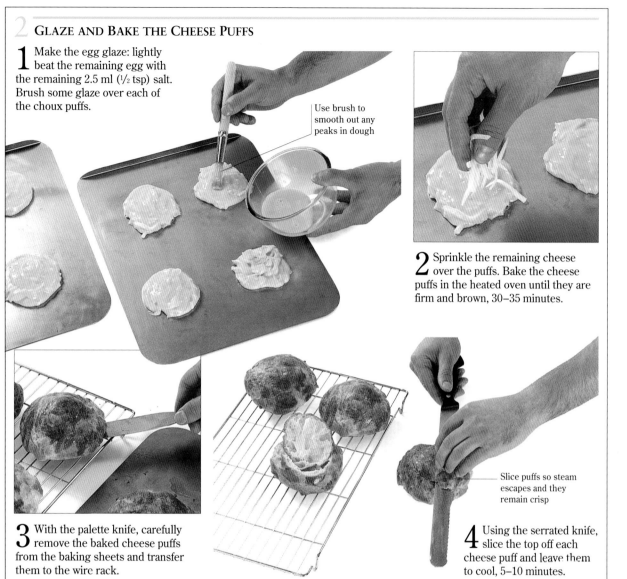

Use brush to smooth out any peaks in dough

2 Sprinkle the remaining cheese over the puffs. Bake the cheese puffs in the heated oven until they are firm and brown, 30–35 minutes.

3 With the palette knife, carefully remove the baked cheese puffs from the baking sheets and transfer them to the wire rack.

Slice puffs so steam escapes and they remain crisp

4 Using the serrated knife, slice the top off each cheese puff and leave them to cool, 5–10 minutes.

MAKE THE FILLING; FILL THE PUFFS

1 Peel the onion, leaving a little of the root attached, and cut it lengthwise in half. Lay each onion half cut-side down on the chopping board and slice horizontally towards the root, leaving the slices attached at the root end. Then slice vertically, again leaving the root end uncut. Finally, cut across the onion to make dice.

2 Set the flat side of the chef's knife on each garlic clove; strike it with your fist. Peel and finely chop the garlic.

3 Discard the tough ribs and stalks from the spinach, then wash the leaves thoroughly.

Remove stringy spinach stalks before cooking

4 Bring a large saucepan of salted water to a boil. Add the spinach, and simmer until tender, 1–2 minutes.

5 Drain the spinach, rinse with cold water, and drain again. Squeeze the cooked spinach or defrosted spinach to remove excess water, then finely chop.

Holding knife with both hands speeds up chopping

6 Slice the smoked salmon into 5 mm x 7.5 cm (¼ x 3 inch) strips. Cut the cream cheese into cubes.

7 Melt the butter in the frying pan. Add the onion and cook until soft but not brown, 3–5 minutes. Add the garlic and nutmeg, salt and pepper to taste, and the spinach. Continue cooking, stirring occasionally, until any liquid from the spinach has evaporated, 5 minutes longer.

8 Add the cream cheese and stir until melted and the mixture is thoroughly combined. Remove the frying pan from the heat.

9 Add two-thirds of the smoked salmon, and pour in the milk. Stir thoroughly, heat 1–2 minutes, then taste for seasoning.

Milk moistens spinach mixture

Smoked salmon cooks slightly in hot mixture

10 Mound 2–3 spoonfuls filling in each cheese puff. Arrange the remaining strips of smoked salmon in a lattice on top.

🍴 TO SERVE

Place a cheese puff on each of 8 individual plates. Rest the lid against the side of each filled puff and serve at once.

Cheese-flavoured choux pastry
forms crisp case

Smoked salmon lattice
makes attractive topping for spinach

CHEESE RINGS FILLED WITH SPINACH AND MUSHROOMS

Mushrooms take the place of smoked salmon in the spinach filling for these cheese rings.

1 Make the choux pastry as directed. Fit a piping bag with a 1 cm (³⁄₈ inch) plain nozzle and fill the bag with the choux pastry.
2 Pipe out a 10 cm (4 inch) diameter ring onto a buttered baking sheet. Pipe out a second ring directly on top of the first. Repeat to make 8 rings. Brush with the egg glaze and bake as directed.
3 Make the filling: omit the smoked salmon. Wipe 375 g (12 oz) mushroom caps with damp paper towels; trim the stalks and thinly slice the mushrooms. Cook the onions as directed, add the mushrooms with the garlic, and sauté until the mushrooms are tender, about 5 minutes; reserve some mushroom slices to garnish the tops of the rings, if you like. Add the spinach to the pan and finish the filling as directed.
4 Using a serrated knife, slice the baked rings in half. Set a cheese ring on each individual plate. Spoon the filling into the bottom half of each ring and set the upper half on top. Garnish with mushroom slices, if reserved.

GETTING AHEAD

The dough and filling can be made up to 6 hours ahead and kept in the refrigerator. Bake the puffs not more than 1 hour ahead. Reheat the spinach mixture and fill the puffs just before serving.

POACHED SCALLOPS IN CIDER SAUCE

🍽 SERVES 6   🥣 WORK TIME 45–50 MINUTES   🍲 GRILLING TIME 2–3 MINUTES

EQUIPMENT

6 scallop half-shells

filleting knife

food processor†

chef's knife

whisk

small knife

slotted spoon

wooden spoon

small sieve

pastry brush

vegetable peeler

piping bag with medium star nozzle

saucepans with lids

potato masher

bowls

lemon squeezer

colander

rubber spatula

†blender can also be used

A creamy cider sauce complements the sweet taste of scallops, which are served in half shells. Piped mashed potatoes flavoured with garlic and herbs complete this pretty dish.

metric	SHOPPING LIST	imperial
500 g	large or Queen scallops	1 lb
2	shallots	2
2	lemons	2
125 ml	cider	4 fl oz
250 ml	water	8 fl oz
125 ml	dry white wine	4 fl oz
30 g	butter	1 oz
30 ml	plain flour	2 tbsp
2	egg yolks	2
125 ml	double cream	4 fl oz
For the garlic-herb mashed potatoes		
500 g	potatoes	1 lb
	salt and pepper	
4–6	sprigs of parsley	4–6
4–6	sprigs of fresh tarragon	4–6
2	garlic cloves	2
60 g	butter	2 oz
2	egg yolks	2
For the egg glaze		
1	egg	1
2.5 ml	salt	½ tsp

INGREDIENTS

scallops

cider

shallots

lemons

garlic cloves

butter

dry white wine

fresh tarragon

parsley

plain flour

potatoes

egg

double cream

egg yolks

ORDER OF WORK

1 PREPARE AND PIPE THE GARLIC-HERB MASHED POTATOES

2 PREPARE AND POACH THE SCALLOPS

3 MAKE THE CIDER SAUCE

4 FINISH THE DISH

1 PREPARE AND PIPE THE GARLIC-HERB MASHED POTATOES

1 Peel the potatoes and cut each one into 2–3 pieces. Put them in a saucepan of cold salted water, cover, and bring to a boil. Simmer until the potatoes are tender, 15–20 minutes.

Herbs, butter, and garlic will enrich mashed potato

Food processor makes puréeing butter very easy

2 Meanwhile, strip the parsley and tarragon leaves from the stalks. Peel the garlic cloves.

3 Put the butter, garlic, and herb leaves in the food processor. Purée until the garlic and herbs are finely chopped.

Tender potatoes mash easily

Fork pierces potatoes easily when fully cooked

4 To test if the potatoes are tender, pierce them with a fork; they should feel soft. Drain the potatoes, then return them to the pan.

5 Carefully mash the potatoes with the potato masher, making sure no lumps remain.

Beat egg yolks into potatoes off heat so yolks cook gradually

6 Beat the herb purée into the potatoes over low heat until the potatoes are smooth, 2–3 minutes. Remove from the heat and beat in the egg yolks, one at a time. Season with salt and pepper. Let cool slightly.

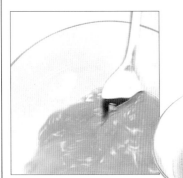

7 Spoon the potatoes into the piping bag fitted with the star nozzle. When full, twist the top until there is no air left in the bag.

8 Pipe the mashed potatoes in rosettes around the edge of each scallop shell.

ANNE SAYS
"Alternatively, spread the potatoes around the shells, making peaks with a fork."

Egg glaze will turn potato rosettes golden brown when brushed over and grilled

9 Make the egg glaze: lightly beat the egg and salt together. Brush the glaze on the potato borders. Set the scallop shells in a grill pan.

Colourful piped potatoes nestle in upward curve of scallop shell

2 PREPARE AND POACH THE SCALLOPS

Cut scallops in even pieces so they cook at same speed

1 If necessary, discard the tough, crescent-shaped membrane at the side of each scallop. Rinse in cold water. Using the filleting knife, cut large scallops into 2 rounds. Leave small scallops whole.

2 Peel the shallots and set each one flat-side down. Slice horizontally, then vertically towards the root, leaving the slices attached. Cut across to make fine dice. Squeeze the lemons; there should be 90 ml (3 fl oz) juice.

3 Put the chopped shallots in a saucepan and add the cider, lemon juice, water, and white wine.

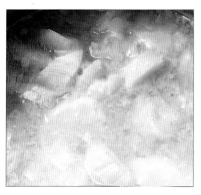

Lightly poached scallops are reserved to be added to finished sauce later

4 Add the scallops and heat just to simmering, then cover with the lid and poach just until the scallops are opaque, 30–60 seconds. Remove the pan from the heat.

5 Lift out the scallops with the slotted spoon and reserve them.

! TAKE CARE !
Do not overcook the scallops or they will be tough.

3 MAKE THE CIDER SAUCE

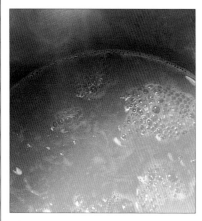

Whisk constantly so flour and butter do not scorch

When mixture foams remove from heat and continue whisking

1 Return the pan of scallop cooking liquid to the heat and bring to a boil. Simmer until it is reduced to about 250 ml (8 fl oz). Remove from the heat.

2 Melt the butter in another saucepan. Whisk in the flour and cook until the mixture foams, 30–60 seconds.

3 Take the pan from the heat, cool slightly, then strain the reduced cooking liquid into it and whisk to mix.

4 Return to the heat and cook, whisking constantly, until the sauce boils and thickens, 1 minute longer. Take the pan from the heat.

Hot sauce will be enriched by egg yolks and cream

5 In a small bowl, whisk together the egg yolks and cream, then add a few spoonfuls of the hot sauce and whisk to mix. Whisk this mixture back into the pan of sauce.

6 Return the pan to the heat and cook gently until the sauce thickens slightly, 1–2 minutes.

! TAKE CARE !
Do not let the sauce boil or it will curdle.

4 FINISH THE DISH

Scallop shells filled on grill pan can be transferred easily to grill

1 Heat the grill. Add the reserved, poached scallops to the sauce with any liquid in the bowl. Taste the sauce for seasoning and adjust if necessary.

Shells are natural containers for poached scallops in sauce

2 Spoon the scallop and sauce mixture into the shells, inside the border of potato rosettes. Grill 7.5–10 cm (3–4 inches) from the heat, until the potatoes and scallops are very hot and browned, 2–3 minutes.

¶O¶ TO SERVE

Transfer the scallop shells to a platter or individual plates and serve immediately.

Potato rosettes form border around scallop shells

V A R I A T I O N

SAUTEED SCALLOPS WITH LEMON-HERB POTATOES

1 Prepare the mashed potatoes as directed, but omit the garlic and egg yolks and beat in the grated zest of 1 lemon with the herb butter. Cover the potatoes with 75 ml (2 ½ fl oz) milk and set in a water bath to keep warm.

2 Heat the oven to low for keeping the scallops warm. Clean the scallops as directed, do not poach them. Omit the cider sauce. Put 30 g (1 oz) plain flour on a sheet of greaseproof paper, season with salt and pepper. Roll the scallops in flour and pat them to discard excess.

3 Heat 30 g (1 oz) butter and 30 ml (2 tbsp) oil in a frying pan. Sauté the scallops, turning them once, until just crisp and brown, 2–3 minutes. Keep warm on a heatproof plate in the oven.

4 Stir the milk into the potatoes; if too thick, add 10–15 ml (2–3 tsp) more milk.

5 Using 2 tablespoons, shape the mashed potatoes into quenelles: scoop out a spoonful of potatoes, then shape into a neat, three-sided oval by turning the spoons against one another.

6 Arrange 3 quenelles on each of 6 individual plates, leaving the centre open for a scallop, omit the egg glaze.

7 Divide the scallops among the plates and serve at once, with lemon wedges for decoration.

GETTING AHEAD

The potatoes, scallops, and sauce can be prepared and assembled in the shells up to 8 hours ahead; keep covered and refrigerated. Grill just before serving, to heat thoroughly.

HERBED SALMON CAKES WITH SWEETCORN RELISH

†◉[SERVES 8 **🥣** WORK TIME 35–40 MINUTES* **🍲** COOKING TIME 15–20 MINUTES

EQUIPMENT

baking dish

food processor†   lemon squeezer

heatproof plate

vegetable peeler

chef's knife   frying pans

small knife

pastry brush

bowls

palette knife

whisk

paper towels

aluminium foil

wooden spoon

large metal spoon

chopping board
†blender can also be used

INGREDIENTS

salmon fillets†   sweetcorn

fish stock   dill

                     celery

vegetable oil

                parsley   olive oil

eggs

lemons   white bread

                              red wine
                              vinegar

mustard   butter   caster
powder   sugar

bottled   pepper
mayonnaise   onion

†four 220 g (7³/₄ oz) cans salmon
can also be used

The delicate, rich flesh of salmon is easily transformed into cakes, served here with tangy sweetcorn relish. The recipe is an excellent way to use up leftover cooked fish.
plus 2–4 hours standing time

metric	SHOPPING LIST	imperial
	butter for baking dish and foil	
2	lemons	2
1 kg	fresh salmon fillet	2 lb
175 ml	fish stock or water, more if needed	6 fl oz
4	slices of white bread	4
1	small bunch of parsley	1
1	small bunch of fresh dill	1
60 ml	bottled mayonnaise	4 tbsp
2	eggs	2
60 ml	vegetable oil	4 tbsp
	For the sweetcorn relish	
1	medium onion	1
1	celery stick	1
1	green pepper	1
500 g	sweetcorn, defrosted or drained canned	1 lb
125 ml	olive oil	4 fl oz
15 ml	caster sugar	1 tbsp
5 ml	mustard powder	1 tsp
	salt and pepper	
75 ml	red wine vinegar	2¹/₂ fl oz

ORDER OF WORK

1 MAKE THE RELISH

2 MAKE THE SALMON CAKE MIXTURE

3 SHAPE AND COOK THE SALMON CAKES

1 MAKE THE RELISH

1 Peel the onion, leaving a little of the root attached, and cut it lengthwise in half. Lay each onion half flat on the chopping board and slice horizontally, then vertically towards the root, leaving the slices attached at the root end. Finally cut across to make dice.

2 Peel the strings from the celery stick with the vegetable peeler. Cut the celery stick across into thin slices.

3 Dice the pepper (see box, right). Put the sweetcorn, onion, and celery, in a large bowl, and add the pepper. Combine the ingredients thoroughly, using the large metal spoon.

Hold corner of chopping board over bowl and scoop with back of knife to transfer chopped vegetables easily

For relish, vegetables should be cut in even-sized dice

HOW TO CORE AND SEED A PEPPER AND CUT IT INTO STRIPS OR DICE

The cores and seeds of peppers must always be discarded.

1 Cut around the pepper core and pull it out. Halve the pepper lengthwise and scrape out the seeds. Cut away the white ribs on the inside of the pepper.

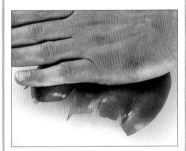

2 Set each pepper half cut-side down on a work surface and press down with the heel of your hand to flatten it.

3 With a chef's knife, slice the pepper half lengthwise into strips. For dice, gather the strips together in a pile and cut across into squares.

4 Put the oil, sugar, and mustard powder in a medium bowl with salt and pepper. Pour in the vinegar.

Red wine vinegar adds bite to relish dressing

5 Whisk the dressing ingredients together and pour over the vegetable mixture.

Dressing will flavour relish ingredients

6 Toss the mixed vegetables in the dressing to mix thoroughly. Season to taste. Cover the relish and let stand at room temperature to let the flavours mellow, 2–4 hours.

2 MAKE THE SALMON CAKE MIXTURE

Paper towels pat salmon lightly dry

1 Heat the oven to 180°C (350°F, Gas 4). Butter the baking dish. Squeeze the juice from 1 lemon.

2 Remove the skin from the salmon fillets, then rinse the salmon in cold water and pat dry.

Surface of salmon is white from sprinkling of lemon juice

3 Arrange the fillets in a single layer in the dish. Sprinkle the salmon with the lemon juice, salt, and pepper. Add enough fish stock or water to half cover the fillets.

4 Brush a little butter over a piece of foil and use to cover the salmon fillets. Poach the salmon fillets in the heated oven, 15–20 minutes.

5 Meanwhile, trim and discard the crusts from the white bread. Put the bread slices in the food processor and work to form crumbs.

Herbs will enhance flavour of salmon cakes

6 Strip the parsley and dill leaves from the stalks, and pile them on the chopping board. With the chef's knife, coarsely chop the leaves.

7 Test if the salmon is cooked. It should just flake easily when pierced with a fork. Remove the salmon from the oven; reduce the oven temperature to low.

8 Drain the salmon, and let cool slightly. Flake the fillets using 2 forks. Pick over the salmon with your fingers, making sure that there are no small bones. Transfer the flaked salmon in a large bowl.

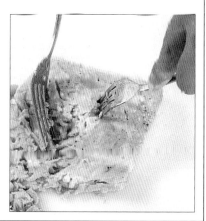

Stir gently wth
wooden spoon so
salmon remains
in flakes

10 Stir the salmon mixture gently but thoroughly with the wooden spoon so the ingredients are combined.

9 Add the mayonnaise, herbs, and breadcrumbs to the salmon. Season with salt and pepper.

11 Lightly beat the eggs. Add them to the salmon cake mixture and stir to combine.

12 To test for seasoning, heat 15 ml (1 tbsp) oil in the frying pan, and fry a little piece of the salmon mixture until brown on both sides. Taste, then adjust the seasoning of the remaining mixture if necessary.

SHAPE AND COOK THE SALMON CAKES

1 Divide the salmon cake mixture into 16 portions. Roll each portion into a ball, wetting your hands if the mixture is sticky. Flatten each ball into a cake, about 1.25 cm (½ inch) thick.

Use wet hands
to roll portions
if mixture
is sticky

! TAKE CARE !
Work gently when shaping the salmon mixture so the cakes will be light.

2 Heat the remaining oil in the frying pan. Add a batch of salmon cakes to fill the frying pan without overcrowding. Fry the salmon cakes over medium-high heat until golden, 3–4 minutes. Carefully turn the cakes over with the metal spatula and brown the other side.

3 Line the heatproof plate with paper towels, and transfer the cooked salmon cakes to the plate to drain. Keep them warm in the oven while cooking the remaining cakes. Cut the second lemon into wedges for serving.

Paper towels absorb excess oil after frying salmon cakes

Salmon cakes served at once are crisp on the outside and moist in the centre

🍽 TO SERVE

Divide the sweetcorn relish between 8 plates and serve 2 salmon cakes on each, with a lemon wedge, and a decoration of celery leaves, if you like.

Relish adds crisp finish to salmon cakes

VARIATION

MARYLAND CRAB CAKES

When we lived in America, and had a summer house in Maryland, we made these cakes with fresh local crabs. Canned crab works well too.

1 Prepare the sweetcorn relish as directed, replacing the green pepper with a red pepper.
2 Omit the salmon fillets. Pick over 1 kg (2 lb) lump crabmeat with your fingers, discarding any cartilage or shell. Prepare the crab mixture as for the salmon cakes. Divide the mixture into 16 portions.

3 Shape the crab cakes, about 1.25 cm (1/2 inch) thick. Fry them as directed.
4 Serve 2 crab cakes per person with the sweetcorn relish. Decorate with dill sprigs, if you like.

── GETTING AHEAD ──

The relish can be prepared up to 4 days ahead and kept, covered, in the refrigerator. The salmon cakes can be shaped up to 4 hours ahead and refrigerated. Fry them just before serving.

STEAMED MUSSELS WITH SAFFRON-CREAM SAUCE

🍽 SERVES 4–6 🥣 WORK TIME 25–30 MINUTES ♨ COOKING TIME 10–12 MINUTES

EQUIPMENT

large casserole with lid

whisk

colander

chef's knife

small knife

bowls

small stiff brush

muslin

medium saucepan

wooden spoon

slotted spoon

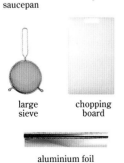
large sieve   chopping board

aluminium foil

INGREDIENTS

mussels

shallots

bouquet garni

saffron

white wine

parsley

double cream

ANNE SAYS
"To save time, you can leave the mussels in both shells."

An echo from the shores of Brittany, these mussels are steamed with white wine, shallots, herbs, and saffron, just until the shells pop open. The natural juices of the mussels add rich flavour to the cooking liquid, which is thickened with cream to form a sumptuous sauce.

GETTING AHEAD

The mussels can be prepared 30 minutes ahead of serving and kept covered with foil. Just before serving, warm them in a 180°C (350°F, Gas 4) oven, 2–3 minutes. Bring the sauce just back to a boil on the stove, coat the mussels, and serve.

metric	SHOPPING LIST	imperial
3 kg	mussels	6 lb
3	shallots	3
250 ml	dry white wine	8 fl oz
1	bouquet garni, made with 5–6 parsley stalks, 2–3 sprigs fresh thyme, and 1 bay leaf	1
1	large pinch of saffron	1
	salt and pepper	
5–7	sprigs of parsley	5–7
125 ml	double cream	4 fl oz

ORDER OF WORK

1 PREPARE THE MUSSELS

2 COOK THE MUSSELS

3 MAKE THE SAUCE AND FINISH THE DISH

1 PREPARE THE MUSSELS

Discard damaged mussels

1 Clean the mussels: scrub each one thoroughly under cold running water with the small stiff brush, then scrape using the small knife to remove any barnacles from the shell.

2 Discard any damaged mussels that have cracked or broken shells and those that do not close when tapped lightly on the work surface.

3 Detach and discard any weeds or "beards" from each mussel.

2 COOK THE MUSSELS

1 Peel the shallots and set each one flat-side down on the chopping board. Slice horizontally towards the root, leaving the slices attached. Slice vertically, again leaving the root end uncut, then cut across to make dice. Chop until very fine.

Bouquet garni is tied to casserole handle

2 Put the wine, chopped shallots, bouquet garni, saffron, and plenty of pepper in the casserole. Bring to a boil and simmer 2 minutes.

Mussels cook with very little liquid

3 Add the mussels to the casserole, cover, and cook over high heat, stirring occasionally, until the mussels open, 5–7 minutes.

! TAKE CARE !
Discard any mussels that have not opened once cooked.

Top mussel shells are easily removed and then discarded

4 Using the slotted spoon, transfer the mussels from the cooking liquid to a large bowl.

5 Discard the top shell from each mussel. Arrange each mussel, in its bottom shell, on a serving plate until all the mussels are on the plate. Cover tightly with foil and keep in a warm place while making the saffron-cream sauce.

Mussels look attractive when arranged in circles on a very large plate

3 MAKE THE SAUCE AND FINISH THE DISH

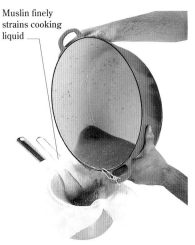

Muslin finely strains cooking liquid

1 Strip the parsley leaves from the stalks and pile them on the chopping board. With the chef's knife, finely chop the leaves.

2 Set the sieve over the saucepan, and line with the muslin. Pour the cooking liquid from the casserole through the lined sieve into the pan. Discard the bouquet garni.

3 Bring the cooking liquid to a boil, and simmer until reduced to about 125 ml (4 fl oz). Pour the double cream into the reduced cooking liquid.

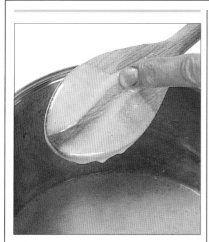

4 Whisk in the cream, and bring back to a boil. Simmer the mixture until slightly thickened, stirring, 2–3 minutes. Allow to cool 1–2 seconds, then lift out the spoon and run your finger across – it should leave a clear trail. Stir in the chopped parsley. Season to taste.

⦿ TO SERVE
Remove the foil and spoon the saffron-cream sauce over the mussels.

VARIATION

MOULES MARINIERE

1 Prepare and cook the mussels in the wine and flavourings as directed.
2 Using a slotted spoon, transfer the mussels to individual soup bowls. Sprinkle with the chopped parsley.
3 Taste the cooking liquid for seasoning. Strain the cooking liquid as directed, and spoon it over the mussels. Serve at once.

VARIATION

CLAMS STEAMED IN WHITE WINE

A departure from the usual mussels, clams are equally delicious steamed in white wine.

1 Scrub 3.5 kg (8 lb) clams in place of the mussels; unlike mussels, clams do not have barnacles or weeds. Cook them as directed with the shallots, white wine, and pepper, omitting the bouquet garni and saffron, allowing 7–10 minutes for the clams to open (thick-shelled clams may take longer).
2 Serve the clams with the cooking liquid, leaving each guest to strip away any black membranes. You may like to serve the clams with a bowl of melted butter for dipping.

Saffron sauce
heightens orange tint of mussels

Chopped parsley
adds texture and vivid green highlights to mouthwatering mussels

SAUTEED ONION AND ROQUEFORT QUICHE

🍽 SERVES 6–8 🥣 WORK TIME 40–50 MINUTES* 🍲 BAKING TIME 30–35 MINUTES

EQUIPMENT

scissors

25 cm (10 inch) flan tin

pastry scraper

pastry brush

frying pan with lid

ladle

chef's knife

chopping board

whisk

strainer

bowls

baking sheet

aluminium foil

rolling pin

wooden spoon

metal skewer

This is my version of a classic quiche from Alsace. The filling of onions, cooked to melting softness, is baked in a pastry shell with a little custard and flavoured with piquant Roquefort cheese.

GETTING AHEAD

The quiche is best freshly baked, but it can be made up to 1 day ahead and kept, covered, in the refrigerator. Warm it in a 180°C (350°F, Gas 4) oven 10–15 minutes before serving.

*plus 45 minutes chilling time

metric	SHOPPING LIST	imperial
2–3	sprigs of fresh thyme	2–3
500 g	onions	1 lb
30 g	unsalted butter, more for foil	1 oz
	salt and pepper	
175 g	Roquefort cheese	6 oz
	For the pastry dough	
200 g	plain flour, more for work surface	6½ oz
1	egg yolk	1
2.5 ml	salt	½ tsp
45 ml	water, more if needed	3 tbsp
100 g	unsalted butter, more for flan tin	3½ oz
	For the custard	
1	egg	1
1	egg yolk	1
125 ml	milk	4 fl oz
1	pinch of ground nutmeg	1
60 ml	double cream	4 tbsp

INGREDIENTS

Roquefort cheese†

onions

double cream

fresh thyme

egg

egg yolks

butter

ground nutmeg

plain flour

milk

† other firm blue cheese can also be used

ORDER OF WORK

1 **MAKE THE PASTRY DOUGH**

2 **LINE THE FLAN TIN**

3 **BAKE THE PASTRY SHELL BLIND**

4 **PREPARE THE ONION FILLING AND BAKE THE QUICHE**

1 MAKE THE PASTRY DOUGH

1 Sift the flour onto the work surface and make a well in the centre. Put the egg yolk, salt, and water in the well.

2 Using the rolling pin, pound the butter to soften it slightly, then add it to the well in the flour. Using your fingertips, work the ingredients in the well until thoroughly mixed.

Your fingertips are ideal for mixing

3 Draw in the flour with the pastry scraper. With your fingers, work the flour into the other ingredients until coarse crumbs form. Press the dough into a ball.

ANNE SAYS
"If the crumbs are dry, sprinkle them with more water before pressing the dough together."

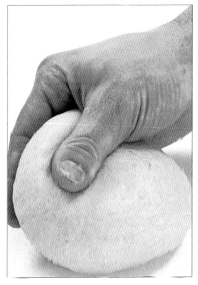

Knead dough with heel of hand until it is very pliable

4 Lightly flour the work surface, then blend the dough by pushing it away from you with the heel of your hand. Gather it up with the pastry scraper and continue to blend until it is very smooth and peels away from the work surface in 1 piece, 1–2 minutes.

5 Shape the dough into a ball, wrap it tightly, and chill until firm, about 30 minutes.

2 LINE THE FLAN TIN

1 Butter the flan tin. Lightly flour the work surface. Roll out the chilled dough to a 30 cm (12 inch) round. Roll up the dough around the rolling pin and drape it over the tin, so that it hangs over the edge.

! TAKE CARE !
Be careful not to stretch the dough or it will shrink when baked.

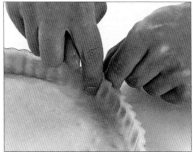

Dough is easy to lift when wrapped around rolling pin

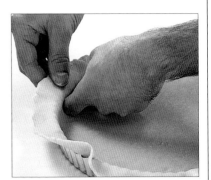

2 Gently lift the edge of the dough with 1 hand and firmly press it into the bottom edge of the tin with the forefinger of the other hand.

3 Roll the rolling pin over the top of the tin, pressing down to cut off the excess dough.

4 With your forefingers and thumb, press the dough evenly up the side, from the bottom, to increase the height of the dough rim.

5 Prick the bottom of the shell lightly with a fork to prevent air bubbles from forming during baking. Chill until firm, at least 15 minutes.

3 BAKE THE PASTRY SHELL BLIND

1 Heat the oven to 220°C (425°F, Gas 7). Line the pastry dough shell with foil, pressing it well into the bottom edge. Trim the foil if necessary so it stands about 4 cm (1½ inches) above the edge of the tin.

Foil helps dough keep its shape during baking

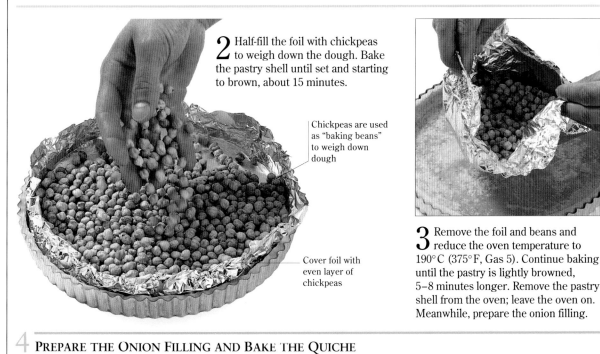

2 Half-fill the foil with chickpeas to weigh down the dough. Bake the pastry shell until set and starting to brown, about 15 minutes.

Chickpeas are used as "baking beans" to weigh down dough

Cover foil with even layer of chickpeas

3 Remove the foil and beans and reduce the oven temperature to 190°C (375°F, Gas 5). Continue baking until the pastry is lightly browned, 5–8 minutes longer. Remove the pastry shell from the oven; leave the oven on. Meanwhile, prepare the onion filling.

4 PREPARE THE ONION FILLING AND BAKE THE QUICHE

1 Strip the thyme leaves from the stalks and finely chop the leaves. Peel the onions, cut in half through root and stem, and slice thinly.

Replace foil and lid after each stirring

Onions should be soft enough to cut with wooden spoon

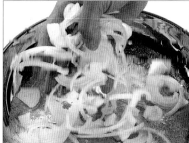

2 Melt the butter in the frying pan. Add the onions and chopped thyme and season with salt and pepper. Butter a piece of foil, press it on top of the onion mixture, and cover with the lid.

3 Cook over very low heat, stirring occasionally, until very soft but not brown, 20–30 minutes.

Ground nutmeg is excellent flavouring with Roquefort and onions

4 Meanwhile, make the custard: put the egg, egg yolk, milk, salt, pepper, and a pinch of ground nutmeg into a bowl. Pour in the double cream.

Cream adds richness to custard

5 Whisk the custard ingredients together until thoroughly mixed.

6 Crumble the Roquefort into a bowl, using your fingertips.

Heat of cooked onions melts Roquefort so mixture is creamy

7 Add the cheese to the softened onions; stir until melted and creamy. Let cool slightly. Using the back of the wooden spoon, spread the onion mixture evenly on the bottom of the pastry shell. Place the flan tin on a baking sheet.

Skewer tests quiche

8 Ladle the custard over the onion mixture to fill the pastry shell almost to the rim, and gently mix in with a fork.

9 Bake the quiche in the heated oven until lightly browned and the skewer inserted in the custard comes out clean, 30–35 minutes. Do not overcook or the custard will curdle. Let cool slightly before unmoulding.

🍽 TO SERVE
Remove the quiche from the tin. Serve warm or at room temperature, cut in wedges. A salad of chicory, watercress, and tomatoes makes a delicious accompaniment.

Crisp pastry holds filling of sweet onions and creamy Roquefort cheese

VARIATION
CABBAGE AND GOAT CHEESE QUICHE
This contemporary version of Sautéed Onion and Roquefort Quiche is filled with cabbage and creamy goat cheese. A soft fresh chèvre log works well, but you can use any type of goat cheese, or even feta if you like.

1 Make, line, and bake blind the pastry shell as directed. Omit the onions. Shred 1/2 small white or Savoy cabbage (total weight about 750 g/ 1 1/2 lb): trim and discard any wilted leaves from the cabbage half. Cut a wedge around the core and remove it. Set the cabbage half cut-side down on a chopping board and finely shred it using a chef's knife. Discard any thick ribs. Cook the cabbage in butter as for the onions, taking care that it does not brown.

2 Make the custard as directed. Cut a 250 g (8 oz) soft goat cheese log into 1.25 cm (1/2 inch) slices. Spread the shredded cabbage over the bottom of the pastry shell and add the custard. Arrange the goat cheese rounds on top of the filling and bake the quiche as directed.

ANNE SAYS
"If the cheese is not brown when the custard is set, brown it under the grill, with a strip of foil over pastry edge."

OYSTERS IN CHAMPAGNE SAUCE

🍽 SERVES 4–6   🥄 WORK TIME 35–40 MINUTES   ☕ GRILLING TIME 1–2 MINUTES

EQUIPMENT

saucepans

bowls

rubber spatula

large metal spoon

whisk

chef's knife

oyster knife

stiff brush

chopping board

The luxurious combination of fresh oysters with Champagne sauce, briefly grilled on the half shell, makes a rich and elegant first course. If you do not have an oyster knife, ask your fishmonger to open the oysters, making sure the juices are reserved for you.

GETTING AHEAD
The sauce can be made up to 30 minutes ahead and kept warm in the bowl, set in a large pan of warm, but not hot, water. Spoon the sauce over the oysters and grill the oysters just before serving.

INGREDIENTS

oysters

Champagne

egg yolks

lemon juice

shallots

butter

rock salt

ANNE SAYS
"Any type of oyster can be used, although the larger, deep-shelled varieties are preferable. Crumpled foil can be used instead of rock salt to hold the oysters steady."

ORDER OF WORK

1   PREPARE THE OYSTERS

2   MAKE THE CHAMPAGNE SAUCE

3   GRILL THE OYSTERS

metric	SHOPPING LIST	imperial
24	oysters in their shells	24
1.15 kg	rock salt, for holding oysters steady	2½ lb
	lemon wedges, parsley sprigs, and tomato strips for decoration (optional)	
	For the Champagne sauce	
4	shallots	4
175 g	butter	6 oz
375 ml	Champagne, about ½ bottle	12 fl oz
4	egg yolks	4
	salt and pepper	
	squeeze of lemon juice	

PREPARE THE OYSTERS

1 With a folded tea towel in 1 hand, grip an oyster shell. Holding the oyster knife in your other hand, insert the point of the blade next to the hinge of the oyster shell. Twist to force the shell open. Cut the top muscle of the oyster from the shell and discard the top half of the shell.

Guard on oyster knife protects your hand

2 Using the blade of the oyster knife, cut loose the muscle from the lower half of the shell.

Oyster shells are perfect cooking vessels

3 Tip the oyster meat with the juice into a small bowl. Reserve the bottom shell. Repeat to open the remaining oysters.

Plump oysters are nestled in their deep shells

4 Scrub the reserved bottom shells clean under cold running water.

5 Spread the rock salt in the grill pan. Arrange the oyster shells on the salt and add the oysters, reserving the juice. Chill the oysters until you are ready to grill them.

Salt holds shells steady in grill pan

2 MAKE THE CHAMPAGNE SAUCE

1 Peel the shallots. Set each one flat-side down and slice horizontally towards the root, leaving the slices attached at the root. Slice vertically and cut across to make fine dice.

2 Melt the butter in a small pan. Skim the froth off the surface; take the pan from the heat and let cool.

3 Put the shallots in another small saucepan and add 300 ml (½ pint) Champagne. Boil until reduced to 30–45 ml (2–3 tbsp). Let cool slightly.

4 Whisk together the egg yolks, oyster juice, and the Champagne mixture in a large heatproof bowl. Set the bowl over a pan of hot, but not boiling, water and whisk until very thick, 5–7 minutes. The mixture should form soft peaks and leave a ribbon trail when the whisk is lifted.

! TAKE CARE !
Do not overheat the sauce or it will curdle; it should thicken gradually.

Bowl should not touch water or sauce will overheat and may curdle

Whisk briskly so butter is emulsified with foaming egg mixture

5 Remove the pan from the heat and whisk the warm butter into the mixture in a slow, steady stream. Leave the milk solids from the butter at the bottom of the pan. Season the sauce with salt, pepper, and lemon juice. Whisk the remaining Champagne into the sauce.

! TAKE CARE !
If the butter is too hot or added too quickly, the sauce will separate.

3 GRILL THE OYSTERS

1 Heat the grill. Spoon 1–2 spoonfuls sauce over each oyster. Grill the oysters about 10 cm (4 inches) from the heat until lightly browned, 1–2 minutes.

Oysters will be lightly cooked beneath creamy Champagne sauce

Be sure oysters are completely covered in sauce

🍽 TO SERVE

Divide the oysters among individual plates and decorate with lemon wedges and parsley sprigs, as well as fine strips of tomato, if you like. Serve at once so sauce is hot and oysters are warm.

ANNE SAYS

"If you don't have oyster plates, prop up the oysters with scooped-out slices of cucumber to hold them steady."

Cucumber slices form "props" for oyster shells

Frothy Champagne sauce coats oysters

VARIATION

OYSTERS ROCKEFELLER

This classic dish, from New Orleans earned its name when it was proclaimed "as rich as Mr. Rockefeller himself".

1 Open the oysters as directed in the main recipe, discarding their liquid. Reserve them on their shells. Omit the Champagne sauce.

2 Peel the strings from 2 celery sticks with a vegetable peeler, then cut each stick into 3–4 pieces. Wash 125 g (4 oz) fresh spinach, discarding any tough stalks, or use 45 ml (3 tbsp) defrosted spinach. Trim 3 spring onions, leaving 2.5 cm (1 inch) of each green top, and cut them across into 3–4 pieces. Strip the leaves from 5–7 sprigs of parsley.

3 Work the celery, spinach, spring onions, and parsley in the food processor until finely chopped. Transfer the vegetables to a bowl.

4 Trim and discard the crust from 1 slice of white bread. Work the bread in a food processor to form crumbs, then mix with the vegetables.

5 Add 175 g (6 oz) softened butter, 2.5 ml (½ tsp) Worcestershire sauce, a dash of Tabasco sauce, salt, and pepper, and combine until smooth.

6 Put 15 ml (1 tbsp) of the mixture on each oyster and grill until the butter is melted and the oysters are heated through, about 5 minutes.

7 Divide among individual plates and decorate with lemon wedges.

RED CABBAGE AND BACON SALAD WITH BLUE CHEESE

🍴 SERVES 6 🥄 WORK TIME 20–25 MINUTES*

EQUIPMENT

bowls

colander

whisk

chef's knife

frying pan

whisk

saucepans

large metal spoon

pepper mill

wooden spatula

chopping board

Red cabbage with strips of bacon and crumbled blue cheese on a bed of lettuce makes a hearty first course for winter, or a tasty lunch for 4 people. I find the contrast in taste, texture, and colour of peppery red cabbage, crunchy bacon, salty blue cheese, and crisp green lettuce especially good.

GETTING AHEAD

The vinaigrette dressing can be made up to 1 week ahead. The cabbage can be prepared and tossed with vinaigrette up to 2 hours before serving.

plus 1–2 hours marinating time

metric	SHOPPING LIST	imperial
½ head	red cabbage (about 750 g/1½ lb)	½ head
60 ml	red wine vinegar	4 tbsp
2 litres	boiling water	3¼ pints
1	small cos lettuce	1
90 g	Roquefort cheese	3 oz
250 g	streaky bacon, cut into thick rashers	8 oz
For the vinaigrette dressing		
60 ml	red wine vinegar, more if needed	4 tbsp
15 ml	Dijon mustard	1 tbsp
	salt and freshly ground black pepper	
175 ml	olive oil	6 fl oz

INGREDIENTS

red cabbage

streaky bacon

cos lettuce

red wine vinegar

Roquefort cheese

peppercorns

olive oil

Dijon mustard

ANNE SAYS
"If you prefer, you can use half olive oil and half vegetable oil when making the vinaigrette dressing."

ORDER OF WORK

1 PREPARE THE VINAIGRETTE DRESSING

2 PREPARE THE CABBAGE

3 PREPARE THE REMAINING INGREDIENTS

1 PREPARE THE VINAIGRETTE DRESSING

Pour oil in slow steady stream when making vinaigrette dressing

1 For the vinaigrette, combine the vinegar with the mustard, and a pinch of salt. Grind in the pepper.

2 Gradually whisk in the oil so the vinaigrette emulsifies and thickens. Taste for seasoning.

ANNE SAYS
"I often make a bottle of dressing in advance and shake it just before using."

2 PREPARE THE CABBAGE

Cored cabbage is ready for shredding

Remove tough core from cabbage

1 Set the cabbage half cut-side down on the chopping board. Trim the stalk end and discard. Peel off any outside leaves that are wilted.

2 Cut the cabbage lengthwise in half. Rest the stalk end of 1 piece on the chopping board; cut out the core and discard. Repeat with the other piece.

3 Finely shred the cabbage quarters with the chef's knife, using your knuckles to guide the knife. Discard any thick ribs. Transfer the shredded cabbage to a large bowl.

4 Heat the vinegar to boiling in the small saucepan. Pour the vinegar over the shredded cabbage and toss to mix so it is thoroughly coated.

Cabbage turns
magenta colour after
being tossed in hot
vinegar and soaked
briefly in boiling water

5 Pour the boiling water
over the cabbage
and let stand until slightly
softened, 3–4 minutes. Drain
thoroughly in the colander,
then return it to the large bowl.

6 Toss the cabbage with enough
vinaigrette to moisten it well.
Taste for seasoning, adding more
vinegar if necessary. Cover the bowl
and marinate the cabbage in the
dressing, 1–2 hours. Meanwhile,
prepare the remaining ingredients.

PREPARE THE REMAINING INGREDIENTS

2 Remove and discard the thick
stalks from the lettuce. Stack the
leaves and roll them up quite tightly.
Cut the rolled lettuce leaves
crosswise into wide strips.

1 Twist off and discard the root
end from the lettuce. Discard any
wilted leaves. Wash the lettuce under
cold running water, then drain the
leaves thoroughly.

Lettuce leaves
are easy to shred
evenly when tightly
rolled in cylinder

3 Crumble the blue cheese into
a small bowl with your fingers,
making sure that the pieces of cheese
are not too small.

4 About 10 minutes before
serving the salad, stack the
bacon rashers; cut crosswise
into strips. Fry the bacon in the
frying pan, stirring occasionally,
until crisp and the fat is rendered
(melted), 3–5 minutes.

5 Spoon the hot bacon and pan juices over the red cabbage, reserving some bacon pieces for garnish. Toss them together.

Marinated cabbage will take on flavour from bacon

Bacon juices are added with crispy bacon pieces

6 Arrange a bed of shredded lettuce leaves on 6 individual plates. Spoon the remaining dressing over the lettuce. Mound the red cabbage and bacon mixture in the centre.

🍽 TO SERVE
Top the salads with the blue cheese and reserved bacon, and serve at once.

VARIATION
WHITE CABBAGE, WALNUT, AND BACON SALAD

White cabbage takes the place of red, and the flavour and texture of walnuts add extra interest to the salad.

1 Make the vinaigrette dressing, substituting half walnut oil and half vegetable oil for the olive oil.
2 Omit the blue cheese. Prepare the cos lettuce as directed. Shred ½ head white cabbage 750 g (1½ lb) as for the red cabbage. Omit the vinegar. Cover with boiling water and let stand until softened, 3–4 minutes. Drain, rinse with warm water, and drain again thoroughly.
3 Coarsely chop 90 g (3 oz) walnuts, reserving some walnut halves for garnish, if you like.
4 Combine the cabbage with the walnuts, then toss with the vinaigrette. Prepare the bacon as directed, pour it over the cabbage with the pan juices, and toss at once. Garnish with the walnut halves, if reserved, and serve on a bed of shredded lettuce leaves.

Brilliant red cabbage is vivid background for crisp bacon and crumbled blue cheese

SZECHUAN SWEET AND SOUR SPARERIBS

⊙I SERVES 6 ⌣ WORK TIME 15–20 MINUTES ⌣ COOKING TIME 1½ HOURS

EQUIPMENT

wok

bowls

small knife

tongs   boning knife

whisk

chopping board

Spareribs are appreciated around the world. In this recipe, they are first browned in a chilli-flavoured oil, then slowly simmered until tender, and coated in a delectable sauce. To make spareribs a main course for 4 people, serve them with boiled or fried rice.

GETTING AHEAD
The spareribs can be cooked up to 1 day ahead and kept, covered, in the refrigerator. Reheat the ribs in a 180°C (350°F, Gas 4) oven 10–15 minutes.

INGREDIENTS

spareribs   sesame oil

chilli purée†

vegetable oil

honey   dark soy sauce

spring onions

dry sherry   cider vinegar

dried red chilli

†crushed chillies can also be used

metric	SHOPPING LIST	imperial
60 ml	dark soy sauce	4 tbsp
60 ml	cider vinegar	4 tbsp
45 ml	honey	3 tbsp
15 ml	sesame oil	1 tbsp
5 ml	chilli purée	1 tsp
60 ml	dry sherry	4 tbsp
1	bunch of spring onions for decoration	1
1.4 kg	spareribs	3 lb
60 ml	vegetable oil	4 tbsp
1	dried red chilli	1
1 litre	water, more if needed	1¾ pints

ORDER OF WORK

1 PREPARE THE SWEET AND SOUR SAUCE AND GARNISH

2 TRIM AND COOK THE SPARERIBS

1 PREPARE THE SWEET AND SOUR SAUCE AND GARNISH

1 In a small bowl, whisk together the dark soy sauce, cider vinegar, honey, sesame oil, chilli purée, and dry sherry. Make the spring onion brushes (see box, right).

Sweet and sour sauce will give rich oriental flavour to spareribs

Aromatic flavours will permeate spareribs

2 TRIM AND COOK THE SPARERIBS

Loose flap of meat is easily removed with sharp knife

1 Using the boning knife, trim any loose flaps of meat and the excess fat from around the spareribs.

2 Cut down through the strips of meat between the bones to separate individual ribs.

ANNE SAYS
"If you are short of time, ask your butcher to prepare the spareribs for you."

HOW TO MAKE SPRING ONION BRUSHES

This is a simple decoration for spicy meats and salads.

1 Trim the roots and most of the green parts from the spring onions, to form pieces that are about 6 cm (2½ inches) long.

2 Make slashes about 2 cm (¾ inch) deep at both ends of each piece. Spread the ends gently to open the slashes.

3 Put the spring onions in a bowl of iced water and chill them until the fringed ends have curled, about 2 hours. Drain the spring onions well before using.

3 Heat the oil in the wok, add the chilli, and cook until it turns dark brown, about 1 minute. Add 3–4 of the ribs and cook over high heat, stirring, until browned on all sides, 2–3 minutes.

Spareribs brown quickly in hot oil

4 Transfer the browned ribs to a plate using the tongs. Working in batches, brown the remaining ribs in the same way. Pour off all but about 30 ml (2 tbsp) oil from the wok.

5 Return all the browned ribs to the wok and pour in enough water so they are completely covered. Heat the liquid until it comes to a boil.

Pour in sufficient water to cover ribs

Chilli remains in wok and adds hot spice to spareribs

6 Reduce the heat and cover the wok. Simmer, stirring occasionally, about 1 hour. The ribs are cooked when the meat shrinks slightly on the bone, and feels tender when pierced with the tip of the small knife.

7 Remove the cover from the wok, remove the chilli, using the tongs and discard.

8 Pour the sweet and sour sauce mixture into the cooked spareribs in the wok. Stir the mixture into the cooking liquid thoroughly to mix.

9 Simmer the mixture, stirring occasionally, until the liquid is reduced to a thick brown sauce, and the ribs are glazed, 25–30 minutes. If necessary, remove the ribs and reduce sauce further by boiling fast.

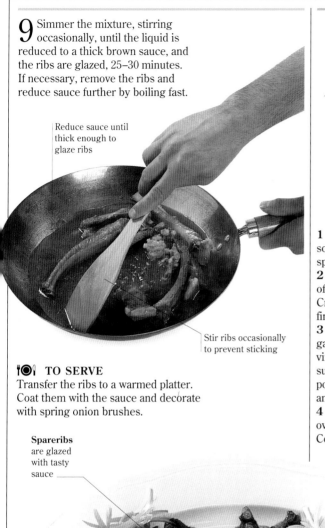

Reduce sauce until thick enough to glaze ribs

Stir ribs occasionally to prevent sticking

TO SERVE

Transfer the ribs to a warmed platter. Coat them with the sauce and decorate with spring onion brushes.

Spareribs are glazed with tasty sauce

Spring onion brushes add oriental touch

VARIATION

INDONESIAN SPICY SPARERIBS

Here spareribs are marinated in a spicy mixture, then simmered in the marinade, which reduces to a deep brown sauce.

1 Omit the sweet and sour sauce. Prepare the spareribs as directed.

2 Peel a 2.5 cm (1 inch) piece of fresh root ginger. Slice, cutting across the fibrous grain. Crush each slice of ginger with the flat of the knife, then finely chop. Peel and finely chop 4 garlic cloves.

3 In a small bowl, whisk together the chopped ginger, garlic, 90 ml (3 fl oz) dark soy sauce, 45 ml (3 tbsp) cider vinegar, 30 ml (2 tbsp) vegetable oil, 30 ml (2 tbsp) brown sugar, 5 ml (1 tsp) ground nutmeg, 5 ml (1 tsp) five-spice powder or ground allspice, 2.5 ml (1/2 tsp) ground cloves, and 2.5 ml (1/2 tsp) ground cinnamon.

4 Put the ribs in a shallow baking dish, pour the marinade over them, and turn the ribs so they are thoroughly coated. Cover and marinate in the refrigerator, turning occasionally, 2–3 hours.

5 Trim 2 spring onions and cut them into thin diagonal slices using part of the green tops.

6 Remove the ribs from the marinade with a slotted spoon and pat dry with paper towels; reserve the marinade. Brown the ribs as directed, omitting the chilli. Pour off all but 30 ml (2 tbsp) oil from the wok, then add the marinade with the water to cover the ribs and simmer them until tender.

7 Boil to reduce the cooking liquid down to a thick sauce.

8 Transfer the ribs to warmed individual plates and spoon a little sauce over them. Sprinkle with the sliced spring onions and serve, decorated with bouquets of fresh herbs.

MEXICAN TURNOVERS WITH CHICKEN AND CHEESE

Quesadillas con Pollo

🍴 SERVES 8   🥣 WORK TIME 35–40 MINUTES   🍲 FRYING TIME 3–6 MINUTES*

EQUIPMENT

chef's knife

palette knife

saucepan   small knife

wooden spoon

slotted spoon

rubber gloves   frying pan

cheese grater

bowls

chopping board

cling film

ANNE SAYS

"Instead of the frying pan, you can also use a griddle for cooking the quesadillas. If it is large enough, cook 2–3 at a time."

These savoury turnovers are a great way to use up cooked chicken. Mild Cheddar makes a good substitute for Monterey Jack cheese.

*total frying time depends on size of frying pan

metric	SHOPPING LIST	imperial
2	medium onions	2
500 g	tomatoes	1 lb
	salt and pepper	
3	fresh hot green chillies	3
4	garlic cloves	4
375 g	cooked boneless chicken	12 oz
60 ml	vegetable oil, more if needed	4 tbsp
125 ml	chicken stock or water	4 fl oz
250 g	Monterey Jack or mild Cheddar cheese	8 oz
12	flour tortillas, each about 15 cm (6 inches) in diameter	12
For the guacamole		
5–7	sprigs of fresh coriander	5–7
1	small ripe tomato	1
1	small onion	1
1	garlic clove	1
1	ripe avocado	1
2–3	drops of Tabasco sauce	2–3
	juice of ½ lime	

INGREDIENTS

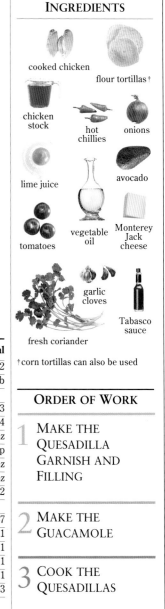

cooked chicken

flour tortillas †

chicken stock

hot chillies   onions

lime juice

avocado

tomatoes

vegetable oil

Monterey Jack cheese

fresh coriander

garlic cloves

Tabasco sauce

†corn tortillas can also be used

ORDER OF WORK

1 MAKE THE QUESADILLA GARNISH AND FILLING

2 MAKE THE GUACAMOLE

3 COOK THE QUESADILLAS

1 MAKE THE QUESADILLA GARNISH AND FILLING

Onion skin lifts off easily with help of small knife

Trim onion but leave root attached

1 Peel the onions, leaving a little of the root attached. Cut lengthwise in half. Lay each onion half flat on the chopping board and slice horizontally towards the root, leaving the slices attached at the root end, then slice vertically, again leaving the root end uncut. Cut across each onion half to make dice.

2 Peel, seed, and chop the tomatoes (see box, page 104). Combine the tomatoes with one-quarter of the chopped onion. Season to taste with salt and pepper; set aside for garnish.

4 Cut the cored chillies into thin rings and reserve for garnish. Core, seed, and dice the remaining chilli (see box, page 106).

Rubber gloves prevent chillies burning your skin

3 Slice off the stalks from 2 of the chillies; remove the cores and seeds with a teaspoon or by tapping the chillies against the work surface.

5 Set the flat side of the chef's knife on top of each garlic clove and strike it with your fist. Discard the skin, finely chop the garlic.

6 Pull the chicken meat into shreds with your fingers, discarding any skin and sinews.

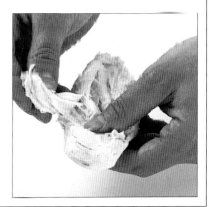

HOW TO PEEL, SEED, AND CHOP TOMATOES

Tomatoes are often peeled and seeded before they are chopped, so they can be cooked to form a smooth purée eliminating the necessity to strain the mixture.

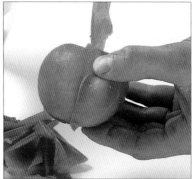

1 Bring a small pan of water to a boil. Cut the cores from the tomatoes. Score an "x" on the base of each tomato. Immerse the tomatoes in the water until the skin starts to split. Transfer them at once to a bowl of cold water to stop cooking.

2 Peel the skin from the tomatoes with the help of a small knife. Cut the tomatoes crosswise in half and squeeze out the seeds.

3 Set each tomato half cut-side down and slice it. Give it a half turn and slice again. Chop the flesh coarsely or finely, as required.

7 Heat 45 ml (3 tbsp) oil in the frying pan. Add the remaining chopped onion, the garlic, and the diced chilli, and cook until the onions are soft but not brown, 2–3 minutes.

8 Add the chicken stock and simmer until almost all the liquid has evaporated, 5–7 minutes. Stir in the chicken and cook 1–2 minutes. Season to taste. Transfer the mixture to a bowl and wipe the frying pan. Grate the cheese.

Shredded chicken takes on flavour from reduced stock

2 MAKE THE GUACAMOLE

1 Strip the coriander leaves from the stalks and pile the leaves on the chopping board. With the chef's knife, finely chop the leaves. Peel, seed, and finely chop the tomato (see box, page 104).

2 Peel and chop the onion and garlic. Place the chopped tomato, coriander, onion, and garlic in a bowl and toss to combine.

3 Cut lengthwise around the avocado, through to the stone. Twist to loosen the halves and pull them apart. With a chopping movement, embed the blade of the chef's knife in the stone and lift it free. Scrape the avocado pulp into the bowl.

ANNE SAYS
"You can take out the stone with a spoon."

Teaspoon scoops all avocado pulp from skin

4 Combine the guacamole ingredients with a fork, mashing the avocado against the side of the bowl. Add a pinch of salt and a few drops of Tabasco.

Ripe avocado pulp will blend easily

5 Add the lime juice and stir well to mix. Taste for seasoning. Cover and refrigerate until serving.

3 COOK THE QUESADILLAS

1 Heat the oven to low for keeping the quesadillas warm. Heat the remaining oil in the frying pan and add 1 tortilla. Sprinkle with about 30 ml (2 tbsp) grated cheese, leaving a 1.25 cm (¹/₂ inch) border. Put about 2 spoonfuls of the chicken mixture on top of the cheese and cook until the cheese begins to melt.

Spoon chicken over cheese in even layer leaving border

HOW TO CORE, SEED, AND DICE FRESH HOT CHILLIES

Fresh hot chillies must be finely chopped so their flavour is spread evenly through the dish. For a hotter flavour you can add the seeds, too. Chillies can burn your skin, so be sure to wear rubber gloves and to avoid contact with eyes.

1 Cut the chillies lengthwise in half with a small knife.

2 Cut out the core and fleshy white ribs and scrape out the seeds.

Slice chilli as thinly as possible

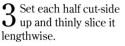

3 Set each half cut-side up and thinly slice it lengthwise.

4 Hold the strips together and cut across into very fine dice.

2 Using the palette knife, fold the quesadilla over in half to enclose the filling. Cook the quesadilla until the tortilla is crispy and golden brown, 1–2 minutes.

3 Turn the quesadilla over and cook until crispy. Transfer to a heatproof plate and keep warm in the oven while cooking the remaining quesadillas, adding oil to the pan as necessary.

🍽 **TO SERVE**

Halve the quesadillas and serve 3 halves on each plate with the guacamole, tomato-onion garnish, and chilli rings. Decorate with coriander, if you like.

Crisp tortillas enclose delicious Mexican filling

Chilli rings add decorative touch

VARIATION

MEXICAN TURNOVERS WITH PORK

Cubes of pork add body to the filling for these quesadillas.

1 Prepare the filling ingredients, but omit the chicken and instead cut 500 g (1 lb) cooked boneless pork into 2.5 cm (1 inch) cubes. Use only 2 hot chillies and dice both of them. Use 60 g (2 oz) Cheddar cheese instead of the Monterey Jack. Chop the leaves from 5–7 sprigs of fresh coriander.
2 Sauté all of the chopped onion with the garlic and diced chillies, then add the pork and cook until browned, 3–5 minutes longer. Omit the chicken stock or water and stir in the chopped tomatoes. Continue cooking until the filling is slightly thick, 5–7 minutes. Taste for seasoning; let cool slightly.
3 Omit the guacamole. Cook the quesadillas as directed, sprinkling each one with 5–10 ml (1–2 tsp) of Cheddar cheese and a pinch of chopped coriander before adding the filling and folding over the quesadillas.
4 Cut the quesadillas into halves and serve decorated with red onion rings and coriander sprigs, if you like.

─── **GETTING AHEAD** ───

The chicken filling can be made up to 1 day ahead and kept, covered, in the refrigerator. The guacamole can be made up to 1 day ahead and refrigerated, tightly covered.

PARMA HAM PIZZAS WITH MOZZARELLA AND BASIL

🍽 MAKES 8 ⏲ WORK TIME 50–55 MINUTES* 🍲 BAKING TIME 10–12 MINUTES

EQUIPMENT

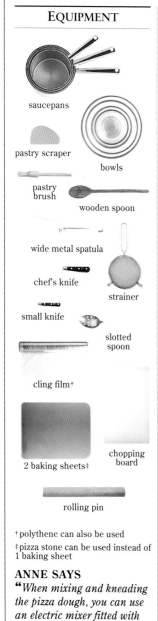

saucepans

pastry scraper

bowls

pastry brush

wooden spoon

wide metal spatula

chef's knife

strainer

small knife

slotted spoon

cling film†

chopping board

2 baking sheets‡

rolling pin

† polythene can also be used

‡ pizza stone can be used instead of 1 baking sheet

ANNE SAYS

"When mixing and kneading the pizza dough, you can use an electric mixer fitted with a dough hook instead of your hands."

Individual pizzas are a welcome opening to any meal. Parma ham, tomato sauce, mozzarella, and fresh basil form the topping for these.

GETTING AHEAD

The pizza dough and tomato sauce can be made up to 12 hours ahead and kept refrigerated. Assemble the pizzas and bake them just before serving.

*plus about 1 hour or overnight rising time

metric	SHOPPING LIST	imperial
	For the pizza dough	
7.5 ml	dried yeast or 9 g (1/3 oz) fresh yeast	1 1/2 tsp
250 ml	lukewarm water	8 fl oz
375 g	strong flour, more if needed	12 oz
30 ml	olive oil, more for bowl	2 tbsp
	salt and pepper	
	For the topping	
625 g	medium tomatoes	1 1/4 lb
1	small onion	1
1	garlic clove	1
15–30 ml	olive oil	1–2 tbsp
22.5 ml	tomato purée	1 1/2 tbsp
1	pinch of sugar	1
90 g	thinly sliced Parma ham	3 oz
375 g	mozzarella cheese	12 oz
1	small bunch of fresh basil	1

INGREDIENTS

Parma ham

fresh basil

mozzarella cheese

olive oil

strong flour

dried yeast

tomatoes

onion

sugar

garlic clove

tomato purée

ORDER OF WORK

1 MAKE AND KNEAD THE PIZZA DOUGH

2 PREPARE THE TOPPING

3 ASSEMBLE AND BAKE THE PIZZAS

1 MAKE AND KNEAD THE PIZZA DOUGH

1 Sprinkle or crumble the yeast over 30–45 ml (2–3 tbsp) of the water in a small bowl; let stand until dissolved, 5 minutes. Sift the flour with 5 ml (1 tsp) salt and 2.5 ml (½ tsp) pepper. Make a well in the centre; add the yeast mixture, remaining water, and oil. Work the ingredients together.

2 Draw in the flour with the pastry scraper and work it into the other ingredients with your fingertips to form a smooth dough.

3 Peel back the dough in one piece, then shape it into a loose ball and turn it 90 degrees. Continue kneading the dough by pushing it away from you and gathering it up into a ball, until it is smooth and very elastic, 5–8 minutes.

Hold 1 end of the dough with 1 hand

Press firmly down into the dough with heel of other hand, pushing it away from you

4 Lightly oil a large bowl. Transfer the dough to the bowl, cover with cling film and let rise in a warm place until doubled in bulk, about 1 hour. Alternatively, leave the dough to rise overnight in the refrigerator.

2 PREPARE THE TOPPING

1 Cut the cores from the tomatoes; score an "x" on the base of each. Immerse in boiling water until the skin starts to split. Transfer to cold water. When cooled, peel and cut each tomato in half; squeeze out the seeds, then chop each half

Coarsely chop each tomato half

2 Peel the onion, leaving a little of the root attached, and cut it lengthwise in half. Lay each onion half flat on the chopping board and slice horizontally, then vertically. Finally, cut across the onion to make dice.

3 Set the flat side of the chef's knife on top of the garlic clove and strike it with your fist. Discard the skin and finely chop the garlic.

Add tomatoes to softened onion and garlic

4 Heat the olive oil in a small saucepan and sauté the onion and garlic until soft but not brown, 1–2 minutes. Stir in the tomatoes, tomato purée, salt, pepper, and a pinch of sugar. Cook, stirring occasionally, until the sauce is thick, 7–10 minutes.

5 With the chef's knife, cut the Parma ham slices across into fairly narrow strips.

Paper-thin Parma ham adds piquancy to topping

6 Thinly slice the mozzarella cheese. Strip the basil leaves from the stalks; reserve some sprigs for garnish.

3 ASSEMBLE AND BAKE THE PIZZAS

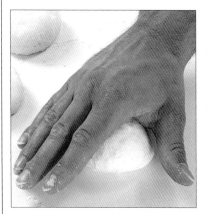

1 Heat the oven to 230°C (450°F, Gas 8) and place 1 baking sheet or a pizza stone near the bottom of the oven. Generously sprinkle the other baking sheets with flour. Knead the pizza dough lightly to knock out the air and cut it into 8 equal pieces. Lightly flour the work surface. Shape 4 pieces of dough into balls.

2 Roll each ball into a round with the rolling pin, then roll and pull each one into a 15 cm (6 inch) round. Transfer to the floured baking sheet.

3 Fold over about 1.25 cm
(¹/₂ inch) of the edge of
each round with your fingertips
to form a shallow rim.

Folding border on
pizza helps prevent
topping from leaking
onto baking sheet

4 Spoon half of the tomato sauce
onto the pizzas and arrange half
of the Parma ham strips on top. Place
2 basil leaves on each pizza and cover
with half of the slices of mozzarella
cheese. Let stand in a warm place until
the dough is puffed, 10–15 minutes.

🍽 TO SERVE
Garnish the pizzas with the reserved
basil sprigs and serve them at once.

Baking pizzas on
preheated baking
sheet ensures that
crust will be crisp

Sprig of basil
echoes herb leaves
under mozzarella
cheese

5 Using the wide spatula, carefully
transfer the pizzas onto the heated
baking sheet. If they stick, chill them
in the freezer 5 minutes first. Bake
the pizzas in the heated oven until the
topping is lightly browned and the
dough is crisp, 10–12 minutes. Shape,
top, and bake the remaining 4 pizzas.

**Fresh
tomato sauce**
tops crisp pizza

TROPICAL PRAWN KEBABS

🍽 SERVES 8 🥄 WORK TIME 20–25 MINUTES* 🍲 GRILLING TIME 4–6 MINUTES

EQUIPMENT

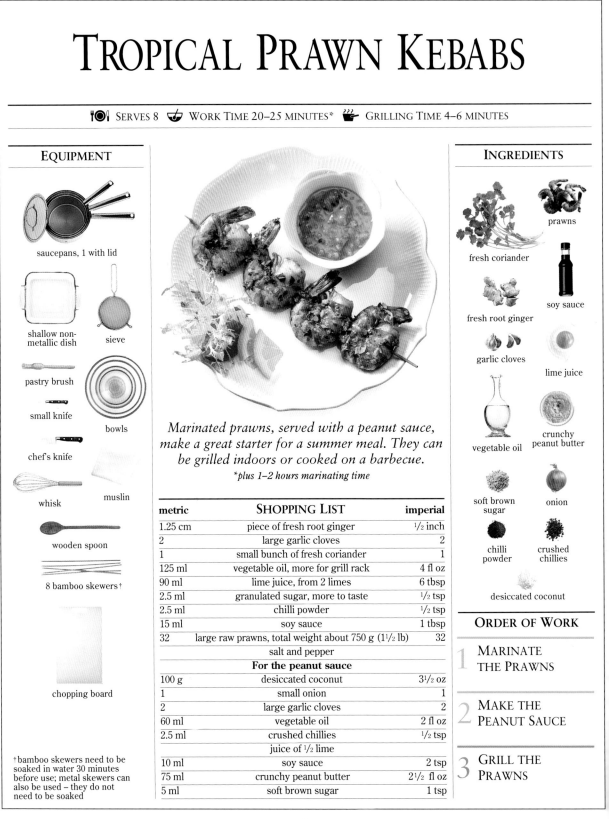

saucepans, 1 with lid

shallow non-metallic dish

sieve

pastry brush

small knife

bowls

chef's knife

muslin

whisk

wooden spoon

8 bamboo skewers†

chopping board

†bamboo skewers need to be soaked in water 30 minutes before use; metal skewers can also be used – they do not need to be soaked

Marinated prawns, served with a peanut sauce, make a great starter for a summer meal. They can be grilled indoors or cooked on a barbecue.
plus 1–2 hours marinating time

INGREDIENTS

fresh coriander

prawns

fresh root ginger

soy sauce

garlic cloves

lime juice

vegetable oil

crunchy peanut butter

soft brown sugar

onion

chilli powder

crushed chillies

desiccated coconut

metric	SHOPPING LIST	imperial
1.25 cm	piece of fresh root ginger	½ inch
2	large garlic cloves	2
1	small bunch of fresh coriander	1
125 ml	vegetable oil, more for grill rack	4 fl oz
90 ml	lime juice, from 2 limes	6 tbsp
2.5 ml	granulated sugar, more to taste	½ tsp
2.5 ml	chilli powder	½ tsp
15 ml	soy sauce	1 tbsp
32	large raw prawns, total weight about 750 g (1½ lb)	32
	salt and pepper	
	For the peanut sauce	
100 g	desiccated coconut	3½ oz
1	small onion	1
2	large garlic cloves	2
60 ml	vegetable oil	2 fl oz
2.5 ml	crushed chillies	½ tsp
	juice of ½ lime	
10 ml	soy sauce	2 tsp
75 ml	crunchy peanut butter	2½ fl oz
5 ml	soft brown sugar	1 tsp

ORDER OF WORK

1 MARINATE THE PRAWNS

2 MAKE THE PEANUT SAUCE

3 GRILL THE PRAWNS

1 MARINATE THE PRAWNS

Chopped leaves
will release
flavour

Whisk together the oil, lime juice,

1 Peel and chop the ginger (see box, page 116). Set the flat side of the chef's knife on top of each garlic clove and strike it with your fist. Discard the skin and finely chop the garlic.

2 Strip the coriander leaves from the stalks and pile them on the chopping board. With the chef's knife, coarsely chop the leaves.

3 Whisk together the oil, lime juice, ginger, and chopped garlic. Add the sugar, chilli powder, chopped coriander, soy sauce, and salt to taste; stir well to mix.

4 Thread 4 prawns on each bamboo skewer, laying each completed skewer in the shallow dish.

ANNE SAYS
"*If using metal skewers, marinate the prawns, then put them on the skewers.*"

5 Pour the marinade over the prawns. Cover and let marinate in the refrigerator 1–2 hours, turning the skewers occasionally. Meanwhile, make the peanut sauce (see page 114).

Distribute
marinade evenly
over prawns

The longer prawns
are left to marinate,
the more piquant
their flavour

2 MAKE THE PEANUT SAUCE

Desiccated coconut is infused in boiling water

1 Bring 250 ml (8 fl oz) water to a boil in a small pan. Stir in the coconut. Cover, and set aside 30 minutes. Meanwhile, finely chop the onion (see box, page 115) and the garlic.

2 Heat the oil in another small saucepan. Add the onion and cook, stirring, until lightly browned, 2–3 minutes. Add the garlic and the crushed chillies and continue cooking until the onion is golden.

! TAKE CARE !
Do not let the garlic brown or it will be bitter.

3 Add the lime juice and soy sauce to the onion mixture; stir to combine. Remove from the heat.

Line sieve with large piece of muslin

4 Stir in the peanut butter and brown sugar. Let cool.

5 Put a piece of muslin in the sieve, set over a bowl. Pour in the coconut and its liquid.

HOW TO CHOP AN ONION

The size of dice depends on the thickness of the initial slices. For a standard size, make slices that are about 5 mm (¼ inch) thick. For finely chopped onions, slice as thinly as possible.

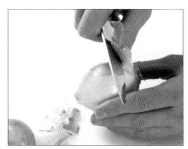

1 Peel the onion and trim the top; leave a little of the root attached to hold the onion together.

2 Cut the onion lengthwise in half, through root and stalk. Place each half cut-side down.

3 Hold the onion half steady with one hand. Make a series of horizontal cuts from the top towards the root but not through it.

4 Make a series of lengthwise vertical cuts, cutting just to the root but not through it.

ANNE SAYS
"When slicing, tuck your fingertips under and use your knuckles to guide the blade of the knife."

5 Slice the onion crosswise into dice. For finely chopped onion, continue chopping until you have the fineness required.

Knuckles guide chef's knife when slicing onion

6 Gather up the ends of the cloth and squeeze the coconut well to extract as much liquid or "milk" as possible. Discard the coconut.

Desiccated coconut yields deliciously perfumed milk when steeped in boiling water

7 Pour the coconut milk into the peanut sauce, and stir until the sauce is evenly mixed. Season to taste with salt and pepper and let stand.

ANNE SAYS
"The peanut sauce may separate on standing. Heat it gently and stir in 1–2 spoonfuls water to re-emulsify it."

3 GRILL THE PRAWNS

Brushing with marinade
keeps prawns moist
during grilling

1 Heat the grill. Brush the
grill rack with oil. Transfer
the kebabs from the dish to the
rack, reserving the marinade
for brushing.

2 Brush the kebabs with
marinade. Grill the kebabs
5–7.5 cm (2–3 inches) from the heat
until they turn pink, 2–3 minutes.
Brush with marinade once or twice
during grilling.

Kebabs are grilled on
rack so excess marinade
drips onto pan

HOW TO PEEL AND CHOP FRESH GINGER

*It is important to chop root ginger quite finely, so the flavour
is released and spread evenly throughout the dish.*

Gather ginger
slices together
with your fingers
as you chop

1 With a small knife, peel the skin
from the root ginger. Using a
chef's knife, slice the ginger, cutting
across the fibrous grain.

2 Place the chef's knife flat on each
slice of root ginger and crush
with your hand.

3 Chop the slices of
root ginger until
they become quite fine.

3 Turn the kebabs and brush again with marinade. Continue grilling until the prawns are pink on the other side, 2–3 minutes longer.

ⅠΟⅠ TO SERVE

Set a kebab on each of 8 plates and accompany with a small bowl of peanut sauce. A few salad leaves, chopped herbs, tomato wedges, and lemon triangles make a colourful decoration.

V A R I A T I O N
VIETNAMESE PRAWN KEBABS

In this alternative to grilled prawn kebabs, the prawns are puréed, then coated with coconut and baked.

1 Omit the marinade and make the peanut sauce, as directed, using 3 chopped garlic cloves.

2 Peel the prawns, reserving 8 in their shells.

3 Make a shallow cut along the back of each peeled prawn and remove the dark intestinal vein.

4 Put the peeled prawns in a food processor with 1 egg, 1 peeled garlic clove, 22.5 ml (1½ tbsp) soy sauce, 22.5 ml (1½ tbsp) Asian fish sauce or 5 ml (1 tsp) anchovy paste, 10 ml (2 tsp) vegetable oil, 15 ml (1 tbsp) plain flour, 2.5 ml (½ tsp) sugar, salt, and pepper. Work to a smooth purée. Transfer to a bowl, cover and chill until firm, 1–1½ hours.

5 Heat the oven to 200°C (400°F, Gas 6). Combine 45 g (1½ oz) desiccated coconut with 30 ml (2 tbsp) dried breadcrumbs on a baking sheet. Wet the palms of your hands and roll the prawn mixture into 2.5 cm (1 inch) balls. Toss in the coconut mixture until coated.

6 Thread the prawn balls onto 8 oiled metal skewers, with 1 reserved unpeeled prawn on each, and lay them on an oiled baking sheet. Bake in the heated oven until the prawn balls are firm to the touch and the whole prawns are pink, 6–8 minutes. Serve at once with the peanut sauce.

7 Introduce splashes of colour to each serving with carrot julienne, lemon twists, and a dill sprig, if you like.

Prawns are served in their shells, leaving guests to peel them at the table

— GETTING AHEAD —
The prawns can be marinated up to 4 hours ahead in the refrigerator. Cook them just before serving.

CHEDDAR CHEESE AND COURGETTE SOUFFLE

🍽 SERVES 6 🥣 WORK TIME 30–35 MINUTES 🍲 BAKING TIME 25–30 MINUTES

EQUIPMENT

2 litre (3¹/₄ pt) soufflé dish

pastry brush

chef's knife

bowls

whisk

grater

wooden spoon

saucepans

sieve

frying pan

chopping board

metal bowl

rubber spatula

Grated courgette and Cheddar cheese give a pleasing green- and orange-speckled appearance to this classic savoury soufflé. Use sharp or mild Cheddar according to your taste. The straight-sided soufflé dish is the key to a successful soufflé.

GETTING AHEAD

The courgette mixture for the soufflé can be prepared up to 3 hours ahead. Whisk the egg whites and finish the soufflé just before baking.

metric	SHOPPING LIST	imperial
500 g	courgettes	1 lb
2	shallots	2
30 g	unsalted butter, more for soufflé dish	1 oz
	salt and pepper	
4	eggs	4
90 g	Cheddar cheese	3 oz
2	egg whites	2
	For the white cream sauce	
175 ml	milk	6 fl oz
30 g	unsalted butter	1 oz
20 g	plain flour	1³/₄ oz
125 ml	double cream	4 fl oz
1	pinch of ground nutmeg	1

INGREDIENTS

courgettes

Cheddar cheese

shallots

unsalted butter

eggs

egg whites

double cream

plain flour

milk

ground nutmeg

ORDER OF WORK

1 PREPARE THE COURGETTES

2 MAKE THE WHITE CREAM SAUCE

3 MAKE THE SOUFFLE BASE

4 FINISH AND BAKE THE SOUFFLE

PREPARE THE COURGETTES

1 Trim the courgettes and grate them coarsely onto a plate.

Courgette skin adds colour to soufflé

2 Peel the outer skin from the shallots and chop them finely (see box, right).

3 Melt the butter in the frying pan. Stir in the shallots and cook over medium heat, until soft, about 2 minutes. Add the courgettes, salt, and pepper and cook, stirring, until the courgettes are just tender, 3–5 minutes.

Do not overcook courgettes or crunchy texture will be lost

4 Transfer the sautéed courgettes to the sieve set over a medium bowl and allow the liquid from the courgettes to drain thoroughly.

HOW TO CHOP A SHALLOT

For a standard chop, make slices that are about 3 mm ($^1/_8$ inch) thick. For a fine chop, slice the shallot as thinly as possible.

1 Peel the outer, papery skin from the shallot. If necessary, separate the shallot into sections at the root and peel the sections. Set each one flat-side down on a chopping board. Hold the shallot steady with your fingers and slice horizontally, leaving the slices attached at the root end.

2 Slice vertically through the shallot, again leaving the root end uncut.

3 Cut across the shallot to make fine dice. Continue chopping, if necessary, until it is very fine.

2 MAKE THE WHITE CREAM SAUCE

1 Scald the milk in a small saucepan. Melt the butter in a medium saucepan. Over the heat add the flour all at once and cook, whisking briskly, until the mixture starts to foam, 30–60 seconds.

Whisk flour vigorously into melted butter

Do not let butter and flour brown

To avoid lumps, whisk constantly when adding milk

2 Remove the pan from the heat and let mixture cool slightly. Then slowly pour in the hot milk, whisking all the time, and continue to whisk until well mixed.

3 Return to the heat and cook the sauce, whisking constantly.

! TAKE CARE !
If the sauce forms lumps at any stage, stop heating and whisk vigorously. If whisking is not sufficient to remove lumps, sieve the sauce.

4 When the sauce boils and thickens, pour in the cream and whisk until thoroughly combined. Season to taste with salt, pepper, and a pinch of nutmeg. Simmer 2 minutes longer. Remove from the heat and set aside.

3 MAKE THE SOUFFLE BASE

1 Separate the eggs. Coarsely grate the Cheddar cheese.

Coarsely grated cheese will melt into hot sauce

2 If necessary, reheat the white cream sauce just to a boil. Remove from the heat, whisk the egg yolks into the hot sauce, one at a time, whisking well after each addition.

3 Return the pan to the heat. Bring the mixture back to a boil, whisking constantly, and simmer 1 minute longer to ensure that the egg yolks are fully cooked.

Sautéed courgettes will blend easily into cheese mixture

Stir grated cheese into sauce off heat so cheese melts but does not form strings

4 Remove the pan from the heat and stir the grated Cheddar cheese into the warm mixture.

5 Stir the drained courgettes into the sauce. Taste for seasoning and adjust if necessary; the soufflé base should be highly seasoned.

4 FINISH AND BAKE THE SOUFFLE

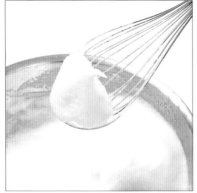

1 Heat the oven to 190°C (375°F, Gas 5). Melt a little butter and grease the soufflé dish using the pastry brush. Reheat the courgette mixture until hot to the touch.

2 Beat the 6 egg whites with a pinch of salt in the metal bowl, using the whisk or an electric mixer until stiff peaks form, 3–5 minutes.

! TAKE CARE !
Do not overbeat the egg whites or they will become grainy.

3 Add about one-quarter of the beaten egg whites to the warm courgette and cheese mixture and gently stir with the rubber spatula until well mixed.

Lightened courgette mixture folds easily into egg whites

Rolling motion ensures mixtures are combined, with minimum loss of volume

4 Add the lightened courgette and egg white mixture to the remaining egg whites in the bowl. Fold the mixture together: cut down into the centre of the bowl with the spatula, scoop under the contents, and turn them over in a rolling motion. At the same time, with your other hand, turn the bowl anti-clockwise. Continue folding until the egg whites are thoroughly incorporated.

Egg whites and soufflé base are thoroughly blended together

Use rubber spatula to scrape soufflé mixture from bowl

5 Spoon the soufflé mixture into the prepared dish. Bake in the heated oven until puffed and brown, 25–30 minutes.

ANNE SAYS
"Don't overcook the soufflé – the centre should be quite soft."

🍴 **TO SERVE**

Serve immediately: plunge 2 large metal spoons into the centre of the soufflé and scoop out a wedge for each serving – it will lose volume within minutes as it cools.

Flecks of green courgette are striking contrast to golden Cheddar

Soufflé is crusty brown on the outside and moist in centre

ONION AND SAGE SOUFFLE

The classic combination of onion and sage is the basis for this soufflé.

1 Omit the courgettes, shallots, and Cheddar cheese.

2 Peel 8 medium onions (about 1 kg/ 2 lb total weight), leaving a little of the root attached, and cut them in half through the root and stem, using a chef's knife. Lay each onion half flat on a chopping board and cut across into thin slices.

3 Melt 45 g (1½ oz) butter in a medium saucepan. Add the onions with salt and pepper, press a piece of buttered foil on top, and cover with the lid. Cook very gently, stirring occasionally, until the onions are very soft but not brown, 15–20 minutes. Remove the lid and foil and cook, stirring, until any liquid has evaporated.

4 Meanwhile, strip the leaves from 5–7 sprigs of fresh sage and pile them on the chopping board. With the chef's knife, finely chop the leaves.

5 Make the white cream sauce as directed.

6 Add the onions and sage to the sauce. Finish and bake the soufflé as directed.

APPETIZERS KNOW-HOW

An appetizer's role in a meal is to whet the imagination as well as the appetite. Full-flavoured ingredients help to achieve this end, in teasingly small portions. No hard and fast rules dictate what the first course of any meal should contain. There are, however, some practical guidelines that will help you select an appropriate appetizer, taking into account the occasion, the type of meal you are serving, the time of year, and the number of people.

CHOOSING APPETIZERS

The appetizer sets the scene for the whole meal, so first consider the dishes that are to follow. If you are serving a hearty main course, you may want to opt for a light and simple appetizer, such as Marinated Goat Cheese Salad or Italian Toasts with Olives, Tomatoes, and Anchovies. Likewise, if the main course is lighter, a more substantial appetizer like Parma Ham Pizzas with Mozzarella and Basil might be more welcome.

If the meal you are serving has more than three courses, you should consider reducing appetizer quantity so your guests do not spoil their appetites. Elegantly diminutive portions can easily be made from recipes such as Herbed Salmon Cakes or Stuffed Mushrooms with Herbs, and a dish like Chicken Liver and Apple Pâté can be served in delicate little egg cups for smaller portions.

Consider also the ambience of the meal you will be serving. For your family and friends, Clams Steamed in White Wine is convivial, served steaming in a big bowl right on the table with plenty of crusty bread for soaking up the juices. Offer the Szechuan Sweet and Sour Spareribs at a casual meal where everyone can leave their knives and forks and use their fingers. If the meal is a more formal affair, look towards Poached Scallops in Cider Sauce served in their shells, or Oysters in Champagne Sauce, or Smoked Trout Mousse with Horseradish and Dill.

Menus may have a theme, carried out from starter to dessert. For example, Spring Rolls with Lettuce and Mint Leaves might be the opening for an oriental dinner, or Steamed Mussels with Saffron-Cream Sauce might create a French bistro mood. Do not hesitate to break away from tradition by mixing and matching themes and cuisines that are compatible. Always keep in mind, however, that a pungent or spicy appetizer should lead into an equally forceful main course, as pepper and spice will dull the palate for more delicate foods to come.

APPETIZERS AND YOUR HEALTH

If you are concerned about calories and fat content, here are some points to consider when preparing appetizers. First of all look for recipes that rely on ingredients naturally low in fat, such as Chinese-Style Stuffed Tomatoes, or Greek-Style Piquant Vegetables. Then turn to dishes containing added fat that can be eliminated; for instance, omit the peanut sauce from Tropical Prawn Kebabs and serve them plain, or with a vinaigrette dressing. Substitute yogurt for the soured cream that accompanies Blini with Smoked Salmon, and reduce the amount of oil that moistens Italian Toasts with Olives, Tomatoes, and Anchovies. In recipes that require pan-frying or sautéing, keep in mind that a non-stick pan will allow you to reduce cooking fat to a minimum. Replace butter with a polyunsaturated oil, such as safflower. In pastry recipes, polyunsaturated margarine can replace butter, although the flavour will be less rich.

PREPARING APPETIZERS AHEAD

The art of entertaining relies on organization, preparing as much as possible in advance so that you can spend more time with your guests. Even for family dinners at home, you will want to be at the table and not at the stove.

For dinner parties, dishes such as Raw Beef Salad with Capers and Chicken Liver and Apple Pâté can be fully prepared, and covered a few hours in advance. Other dishes, such as Stuffed Vine Leaves, Greek-Style Piquant Vegetables, and Smoked Trout Mousse with Horseradish and Dill, can be completed at least a day in advance and left covered in the refrigerator, to be transferred to serving bowls, or unmoulded onto plates just before serving. These appetizers are as appropriate for a buffet as for a sit-down meal.

Other recipes may require quick reheating before being brought to the table, but they too can be made a day ahead: Sautéed Onion and Roquefort Quiche, Szechuan Sweet and Sour Spareribs and Stuffed Mushrooms with Herbs are in this category, to name a few. No recipes have to be prepared totally at the last minute. At the very least, certain parts of cooking and assembly can be done in advance, such as chopping vegetables or making pastry shells, freeing you to take care of other things before the meal is served. So before you embark on an appetizer, read the section on Getting Ahead carefully to be sure that the preparation plan it describes fits into your schedule.

MICROWAVE COOKING

Many of these recipes can be adapted for microwave cooking, speeding up their preparation. For Stuffed Vine Leaves, for example, you can toast the pine nuts, prepare the rice stuffing, and cook the stuffed leaves in the microwave. Cooking time for Stuffed Mushrooms with Herbs is greatly reduced by using the microwave. Greek-Style Piquant Vegetables can be microwaved, and Clams Steamed in White Wine can be steamed open in the microwave.

In other recipes, you can prepare ingredients quickly in the microwave oven. The salmon fillet for Herbed Salmon Cakes can be poached in the microwave, although the cakes themselves are best cooked on top of the stove for a golden, crispy exterior. In Sautéed Onion and Roquefort Quiche, the onions cook quickly in the microwave, and you can rapidly wilt the cabbage for Cabbage and Goat Cheese Quiche.

Don't forget that some basic techniques are easy in the microwave. You can peel the skin from onions, garlic, and tomatoes: heat onions and garlic cloves at High (100% power); put tomatoes in boiling water in a microwave-safe bowl and cook until the skin splits. You can also cook bacon and even proof yeast dough in the microwave.

HOW-TO BOXES

Some basic techniques appear in a number of recipes and they are shown in extra detail in these special "how-to" boxes:

CHICKEN STOCK

🍽️ MAKES ABOUT 2 LITRES (3½ PINTS)

🥣 WORK TIME 15 MINUTES

🍲 COOKING TIME UP TO 3 HOURS

SHOPPING LIST

1.15 kg	chicken backs and necks	2 2½ lb
1	onion, quartered	1
1	carrot, quartered	1
1	celery stick, quartered	1
1	bouquet garni	1
5	peppercorns	5
2 litres	water, more if needed	3½ pints

1 Put the chicken pieces in a large saucepan with the remaining ingredients and cover with water.

2 Bring to a boil. Simmer up to 3 hours, skimming occasionally with a large metal spoon.

3 Strain the stock into a large bowl. Cool, then cover, and keep in the refrigerator.

FISH STOCK

🍽️ MAKES ABOUT 1 LITRE (1¾ PINTS)

🥣 WORK TIME 10–15 MINUTES

🍲 COOKING TIME 20 MINUTES

SHOPPING LIST

500 g	fish bones and heads, cut into 5 cm (2 inch) pieces	1 lb
1	onion, thinly sliced	1
250 ml	dry white wine	8 fl oz
1 litre	water	1¾ pints
3–5	sprigs of parsley	3–5
5 ml	peppercorns	1 tsp

1 Wash the fish bones and heads; place them in a medium saucepan with the remaining ingredients.

2 Bring to a boil and simmer 20 minutes, skimming occasionally with a large metal spoon.

3 Strain the stock into a bowl. Cool, then cover, and keep in the refrigerator.

INDEX

ACKNOWLEDGEMENTS

Photographers David Murray
Jules Selmes
Photographer's Assistant Ian Boddy

Chef Eric Treuille
Cookery Consultant Annie Nichols
Assisted by Jane Stevenson

Typesetting Linda Parker
Text film by Disc to Print (UK) Limited

Production Consultant Lorraine Baird

*Carroll & Brown Limited
would like to thank ICTC
(0181 568-4179) for supplying the
Cuisinox Elysee pans used throughout the
book and The Kitchenware Merchants
Limited for the Le Creuset cookware.*

*Anne Willan would like to thank her
chief editor Kate Krader, associate editors
Stacy Toporoff and Jacqueline Bobrow,
and consultant editor Cynthia Nims, for
their vital help with writing this book
and researching and testing the recipes,
aided by La Varenne's chefs and trainees.*

NOTES

- Metric and imperial measures have been calculated separately. Only use one set of measures as they are not exact equivalents.

- All spoon measurements are level.

- Spoon measurements are calculated using a standard 5 ml teaspoon and 15 ml tablespoon to give an accurate measurement of small amounts.